The Fourteenth Amendment

Equal Protection Under the Law

The
Constitution

David L. Hudson, Jr.

Enslow Publishers, Inc.

40 Industrial Road   PO Box 38
Box 398   Aldershot
Berkeley Heights, NJ 07922   Hants GU12 6BP
USA   UK

http://www.enslow.com

To Carla

Library of Congress Cataloging-in-Publication Data

Hudson, David (David L.), 1969-
    The Fourteenth Amendment : equal protection under the law / David L. Hudson, Jr.
        p. cm. — (The constitution)
    Includes bibliographical references and index.
    ISBN 0-7660-1904-7
    1. United States. Constitution. 14th Amendment—Juvenile literature. 2. African Americans—Civil rights—Juvenile literature. 3. Equality before the law—United States—Juvenile literature. 4. Due process of law—United States—Juvenile literature. I. Title. II. Constitution (Springfield, Union County, N.J.)
KF4757 .H83   2002
342.73'085—dc21

                                        2001004121

Printed in the United States of America

10 9 8 7 6 5 4 3 2

To Our Readers: We have done our best to make sure all Internet addresses in this book were active and appropriate when we went to press. However, the author and the publisher have no control over and assume no liability for the material available on those Internet sites or on other Web sites they may link to. Any comments or suggestions can be sent by e-mail to comments@enslow.com or to the address on the back cover.

Illustration Credits: Corbis/Bettman, p. 82; Courtesy of Frank Lewis, p. 55; Courtesy of the Office of Public Relations, Virginia Military Institute, Lexington, VA, p. 90; Culver Pictures, Inc., p. 20; *The Dallas Morning News*/David Leeson, p. 66; John Grafton, *The American Revolution: A Picture Sourcebook* (New York: Dover Publications, Inc., 1975), p. 6; *The Kansas City Star*, p. 72; Library of Congress, pp. 13, 75; National Archives, pp. 7, 26, 49; The New York Public Library, p. 80; Photograph by Dane Penland, Smithsonian Institution, Courtesy of the Supreme Court of the United States, p. 88; Reproduced from the *Dictionary of American Portraits*, Published by Dover Publications, Inc., in 1967, pp. 16, 17, 19, 22, 27, 30, 31, 39.

Cover Illustration: Associated Press.

Contents

1

The Second Bill of Rights

"**W**e hold these Truths to be self-evident, that all Men are created equal." So states the Preamble to the most important document in America's history—the United States Constitution. America was founded on freedom, equality and democracy and Americans still pride themselves on those qualities today. Both the Constitution and the Bill of Rights (the first ten amendments to the Constitution) describe the United States as a country that treats its citizens equally. These documents are shining examples of the American democratic system. But the high ideal that "all men are created equal" has not represented reality, especially for African Americans and women. American freedom has been both a reality and a mythic ideal—a living truth for millions of Americans; a cruel mockery for others.[1]

Not all people came to the United States of their own free will. Beginning in 1619, Africans were brought to North America in chains and treated as the property of white people.

Women, too, were excluded from American equality. Early American women were not mentioned in the Declaration of Independence, they were absent in the

Constitution, they were invisible in the new political democracy.[2] Married women could not sue in their own name or sign contracts. They were not even allowed to vote until 1920.

The Declaration of Independence and the United States Constitution did not live up to their promise of equality and freedom. However, after a bloody Civil War, (1861–1865), a series of amendments to the Constitution were intended to provide greater equality for the people. One was the Fourteenth Amendment. United States Supreme Court Justice John Paul Stevens said, the Fourteenth Amendment and its two related Civil War amendments "breathed new life into the entire document" of the Constitution.[3] The Fourteenth Amendment was so important, in fact, that it has been called a second Bill of Rights and a second American Revolution.

The amendment permanently changed American constitutional law. It prevented state government officials from abusing people's liberty. When the Founding Fathers first wrote the Constitution, their main concern was to ensure that a national government would not overwhelm the freedoms of the states. The central government had to be restrained or it might seem to be acting like the English Parliament and King George III did when dealing with the American colonists before the Revolutionary War. To protect the people, the Founding Fathers added ten amendments to the Constitution, known as the Bill of Rights. The first eight amendments guarantee that the federal government will not trample on certain individual liberties, such as freedom of speech and religion.

However, the Bill of Rights restrained only the federal government, not the various state and local

King George III and the English Parliament did not protect
the rights of the American colonists.

governments. Most American citizens come into contact much more often with various state and local officials than with federal officials. This was especially true in early American history when the federal government was much smaller than it is now. To put this into perspective, think about how many times you have seen or spoken with a local police officer. Compare that with how many times you have seen a

The Bill of Rights that was added to the Constitution restrained the federal government, but not the governments of the states.

member of the Federal Bureau of Investigation (FBI) or the Central Intelligence Agency (CIA). By far, most people have more involvement with state and local officials than federal ones. Yet, many of the Founding Fathers did not appreciate the fact that the greatest dangers to liberty can come from state and local officials. They may have assumed that state constitutions would provide adequate protection. This was not the case, however, particularly for women and African Americans. Many lawmakers came to believe that the United States Constitution needed to make sure that the freedoms protected in the Bill of Rights would also be protected against the states. The Fourteenth Amendment extends the protections of the Bill of Rights to possible abuses by state and local officials. The Fourteenth Amendment breathed new life into American constitutional law. As leading television producer and author Fred W. Friendly said, "It was as if the Congress had held a second constitutional convention, and created a federal government of vastly expanded proportions."[4]

To appreciate the importance of the Fourteenth Amendment, consider the following example. A public school student wears a shirt to school that supports the Green party and its presidential candidate, Ralph Nader. The school has a dress code but it only prohibits student expression that is disruptive or indecent. An assistant school principal, who believes the Green party nominee Ralph Nader cost the Democratic party the presidency in the November 2000 election, becomes upset. He immediately suspends the student for three days for disruptive conduct. School officials fail to give the student notice of the charge against him and offer him no fair hearing before imposing the discipline. The student does not have an opportunity to contest the suspension until the next month, when the school board holds its next meeting.

In this example, the public school officials violated several constitutional rights of the student. Even though students and minors have fewer constitutional rights than adults, the United States Supreme Court has stated that students do not lose their constitutional rights at the "schoolhouse gate."[5] The assistant school principal violated the student's rights to engage in political speech under the First Amendment. However, without the Fourteenth Amendment, the school official, because he is not a federal officer, can act however he chooses without running afoul of the federal Constitution. The student may be able to sue under the state constitution, but without the Fourteenth Amendment there would be no claim under the federal constitution.

In any case that involves an alleged violation of a constitutional right by a non-federal government official, the Fourteenth Amendment comes into play. It is a vital part of the Constitution, helping to provide school students and all American citizens with the protections contained in the Bill of Rights.

The Five Sections of the Fourteenth Amendment

2

The Fourteenth Amendment has five sections. Today, only two of them are important: the first and the fifth. The second, third, and fourth sections all deal with managing the Southern states that had left the Union before the Civil War.

The heart of the Fourteenth Amendment is its first section. It contains perhaps the two most important phrases in American constitutional law—due process and equal protection. Due process means that the government must act according to the law. Equal protection means that all people must be treated the same under the law. The first section of the Fourteenth Amendment reads:

> All persons born or naturalized in the United States, and subject to the jurisdiction thereof, are citizens of the United States and of the State wherein they reside. No State shall make or enforce any law which shall abridge the privileges and immunities of citizens of the United States; nor shall any State deprive any person of life, liberty, or property, without due process of law; nor deny to any person within its jurisdiction the equal protection of the laws.

The first sentence, which defines citizenship, overturned the U.S. Supreme Court's 1857 decision in the case *Dred Scott* v. *Sandford,* which said that African Americans were not and could not be citizens, and "had no rights that the white man was bound to respect."[1] One of the main reasons the Fourteenth Amendment was written was to show that African Americans were, in fact, citizens of the United States.

Privileges and Immunities

The second clause of the section contains the so-called "privileges and immunities clause." It says: "No State shall make or enforce any law which shall abridge the privileges or immunities of citizens of the United States." The meaning of this clause has often been the subject of intense debate among legal scholars. Some argue that the phrase "privileges and immunities" was intended to extend the provisions in the Bill of Rights to the states. Others view the clause as much more limited.

In 1873, the Supreme Court interpreted the privileges and immunities clause very narrowly. The Court ruled that the privileges and immunities clause applied only to certain rights people had as citizens of the federal government, or national citizens. The Court said that the states did not have to provide its citizens the same "privileges and immunities" as the federal government provided national citizens. The ruling meant that the Fourteenth Amendment did not automatically extend the protections of the Bill of Rights to the states. It would take Supreme Court decisions throughout the twentieth century to change that.

Due Process and Equal Protection

The last two clauses of Section One of the Fourteenth Amendment are very important. They are the due process and equal protection clauses. Due process, a principle that came from English law, means that the government must obey the law and act in a reasonable fashion. Today, due process is divided into two concepts: procedural due process and substantive due process.

Procedural due process means that the state must use fair procedures when it acts to limit a person's life, liberty or property. Substantive due process, on the other hand, means that the actual provisions of the law must be reasonable.

Equal protection means that the government may not pass a law that discriminates against an individual or group of society. For example, a law prohibiting interracial marriages treats people differently based on race and thus violates the equal protection clause.

Section Two of the Fourteenth Amendment was added to make sure that African Americans would have the right to vote. The section provided that all males twenty-one years of age and older could vote. If any male, twenty-one or older, was denied the right to vote, then the state refusing to allow him to vote would lose some of its congressional seats. Because of these developments, two African Americans in the Reconstruction period were elected United States Senators and twenty were elected to the House of Representatives.[2] Unfortunately, after Reconstruction ended and Northern troops left the South, many whites, particularly in the South, again made it difficult for African Americans to vote. Polling places were set up far away from African-American communities. Sometimes whites used violence and intimidation to prevent African Americans from voting.[3] The Fourteenth Amendment gave the courts the means to enforce equal treatment to all Americans. It would

After Reconstruction ended, many whites made it difficult for African Americans to exercise their voting rights.

take time, however, before those means would be used to full effect.

Section Three prohibited ex-Confederates from serving in Congress. The intention was to prevent those who had waged war against the American Union from being its new leaders.

Section Four said that slaveholders could not claim compensation for their recently freed slaves.

Although the Fifth Amendment said citizens must be paid a fair price when their property was taken away by the government, the government refused to recognize slaves as such property. It also declared illegal Confederate war debt claims.

Section Five gave Congress the power to pass any other needed laws to protect the due process and equal protection rights of Americans. This meant it would be assumed that Congress could make laws to better enforce the Fourteenth Amendment.

The Need for the Fourteenth Amendment

In 1791, the states ratified, or officially approved, ten amendments to the United States Constitution. These became known as the Bill of Rights. The Bill of Rights safeguarded individual liberties from any overreaching actions by the federal government.

However, in considering the amendments, the U.S. Senate had dropped one of the original proposals that James Madison, the man known as the "Father of the Bill of Rights," considered the most important. That proposal provided: "No state shall violate the equal rights of conscience, or the freedom of the press, or the trial by jury in criminal cases."[1] Madison said this proposal was vital because, "there is more danger of those powers being abused by the state governments than by the government of the United States."[2] At the time the Bill of Rights was adopted, the state governments were very powerful. Madison feared it was the states, not the national government, that were most likely to infringe on the rights of individual citizens. By dropping this proposed amendment on September 7, 1789, the Senate gave up protection of individual liberty against state governments. Any protection would fall largely to the various state constitutions.

Barron *v.* Baltimore

In 1833, the United States Supreme Court ruled in *Barron* v. *Baltimore* that the Bill of Rights did not apply to state or local governments.[3] John Barron, who owned a wharf in Baltimore, claimed that city officials had violated his constitutional rights when one of their construction projects damaged his property. In 1815, Barron purchased his dock in Fell's Point in Baltimore, a harbor that had been home to the country's first naval ships. The wharves of Barron and their owners were hurt by the road-building and soil-excavating activities approved by city officials. One wharf owner, Hezekiah Waters, wrote to the city officials in 1817 to protest the damage being done by the city's continued digging to build roads. His letter read:

> For within one year last past, many parts of Our Wharves have been filled up with sand and dirt from four to six feet. We apprehend, and fear, that if the City Commissioners continue digging ditches to alter the Water Course . . . that Our Wharves will be useless to us, and entirely ruined.[4]

In 1822, Barron hired a lawyer. Barron's lawyer argued that the city officials had violated the Fifth Amendment of the Constitution by taking away Barron's property through destruction without giving him just compensation (fair payment). Barron wanted the city to pay for the damage done to his dock. City officials,

James Madison became known as the "Father of the Bill of Rights."

In the case of Barron v. Baltimore, *the Supreme Court, led by Chief Justice John Marshall, ruled in favor of the city.*

however, countered that they were acting for the general welfare of the city by improving the city streets, a fair use of their power.

In 1828, a jury awarded Barron $4,500 in damages. In December 1830, however, a court of appeals reversed the jury verdict. The appeals court declared that the decision violated the Constitution. Barron appealed his case all the way to the United States Supreme Court in what would become the first test case of the Bill of Rights. Charles F. Mayer argued for Barron and Maryland Attorney General Roger B. Taney made the case for Baltimore. Unfortunately for John Barron, the Supreme Court, led by Chief Justice John Marshall, ruled in favor of the city. To Marshall, the question was of "great importance, but not of much difficulty." Marshall pointed out that each state had established its own constitution to limit the powers of its government "as its judgment dictated."[5] Maryland's constitution did not have a provision that protected private property from state interference the way the Fifth Amendment protected against the national government. Marshall reasoned that if the Founding Fathers had intended for the Bill of Rights to apply to the states, then "they would have declared this purpose in plain and intelligible language."[6] Instead, the Fifth Amendment is "intended solely as a limitation on the exercise of power by the government of the United States and is not applicable to the legislation of the states."[7] Marshall concluded that the Supreme Court had no jurisdiction in the matter, which was a local and not a national affair, and dismissed Barron's lawsuit.

The ruling in *Barron* v. *Baltimore* meant that American citizens could sue for constitutional violations only if the violators were federal government officials. As one author put it, "It would take a civil war and another century of judicial theorizing to change that interpretation."[8] It would also take the adoption of the Fourteenth Amendment.

The Debate Over Slavery

Beginning in 1619, slaves from Africa were imported into North America. Slavery became a staple of early American life, particularly in the South where slaves were put to work tending cash crops in huge plantations. From the beginning of the American republic, slavery was a thorny issue. It was the source of many heated debates—both moral and political. Slavery became an even hotter topic in 1819 when the state of Missouri petitioned Congress to become a state. Because Missourians held slaves their membership in Congress would upset the balance between free states and slave states. Politicians on both sides had strong feelings over the issue.

Kentucky Congressman Henry Clay helped forge the so-called Missouri Compromise of 1820. Under this plan, Missouri became a slave state and Maine entered the Union as a free state. The compromise, which was aimed at maintaining a balance between slave and free states, also prohibited slavery in lands of the Louisiana Territory above Missouri's southern border. Any future states to be carved out of that

Henry Clay of Kentucky helped forge the Missouri Compromise of 1820 which aimed to maintain a balance between slave states and free states.

region would have to be free. The compromise settled the political debate temporarily, but it did nothing to stop the moral struggle over slavery. People who opposed slavery called themselves abolitionists. They worked to varying degrees to expose the institution as abhorrent and immoral. Frederick Douglass, who rose out of slavery to become a leading abolitionist, speaker and writer, said that the Constitution was "conceived in sin and shaped in iniquity."[9] He and others argued over slavery in newspapers and other public forums. Their debate over slavery reached the Supreme Court with the case of a slave named Dred Scott.

The Dred Scott Decision

Not much is known about the slave, Dred Scott, even though he is perhaps more famous than any "individual litigant in American constitutional history."[10] Peter Blow, Scott's owner, moved from Alabama to Missouri in 1832. After his death, the executor of Blow's estate (person responsible for the deceased person's property) sold Scott to Dr. John Emerson, an army doctor who lived in St. Louis, Missouri.

In 1834, Emerson moved his family, and Scott, to the free state of Illinois. Some time later, Emerson relocated to what was then known as the Wisconsin

The Court ruled that Dred Scott was still a slave in the state of Missouri.

Territory, which also outlawed slavery. In 1842, Emerson moved back to St. Louis and died a year later.

In 1846, Dred Scott and his wife Harriet filed lawsuits in Missouri state courts, claiming that they had been emancipated, or freed, when Emerson took them into "free" territory. Emerson's widow and her brother John Sanford contested Dred Scott's suit and the case eventually reached the Supreme Court.

The Scotts seemed to have the law on their side. The legal doctrine of the day was "once free, always free."[11] Some slaves who had moved to free states or territories had, in fact, obtained their freedom. However, Missouri politics and the addition of more proslavery judges on the Missouri Supreme Court doomed Scott before the state's highest court.[12]

At the time the case was heard, the Supreme Court was made up of a majority of Southerners who held proslavery views. On March 6, 1857, the Court ruled 7-2 that Dred Scott was still a slave in Missouri. The lead opinion was written by Chief Justice Roger B. Taney, the same man who represented the city of Baltimore in the earlier case of *Barron* v. *Baltimore.*

Taney wrote that African Americans "were not intended to be included under the word 'citizens' in the Constitution, and can therefore claim none of the rights and privileges which that instrument provides for and secures to citizens of the United States." Taney referred to African Americans as "that unfortunate race" who were considered "so far inferior, that they had no rights which the white man was bound to respect." In his opinion Taney recognized that the words of the Declaration of Independence—"that all men are created equal"— would seem to embrace the whole human family. However, he reasoned, "But it is too clear for dispute, that the enslaved African race

Chief Justice Roger B. Taney declared the Missouri Compromise unconstitutional in the Dred Scott ruling.

were not intended to be included, and formed no part of the people who framed and adopted" the Declaration of Independence.[13]

The court could have simply ruled that when Scott returned to Missouri, a slave state, he became a slave. However, Taney went much further. He declared the Missouri Compromise of 1820 unconstitutional, saying that Congress did not have the power to outlaw slavery in new territories. This ruling helped intensify divisions between slave and free states and lead the United States to the Civil War.

Justices John McLean and Benjamin Curtiss dissented. McLean pointed out that many African Americans were "citizens of the New England States" and had the right to vote.[14] McLean wrote that "a belief was cherished by the leading men, South as well as North, that the institution of slavery would gradually decline, until it would become extinct."[15] McLean also pointed out that slavery had existed throughout the world and was not confined to people of African descent. "On the same principles, white men were made slaves," he wrote. "All slavery has its origin in power, and is against right."[16] Toward the end of his opinion, McLean warned that if a Missouri state court could ignore existing law then "what protection do the laws afford?"[17]

Abolitionists and others who opposed slavery were angered by the Court's decision. Many politicians were outraged that Taney struck down the Missouri Compromise of 1820. It was the compromise that had eased tensions over the spread of slavery for many years. An Illinois politician by the name of Abraham Lincoln emerged as a leading figure in the debate over this issue of whether slavery would be permitted to spread to new territories.

Lincoln criticized the Dred Scott decision and called for its reversal. In 1858 he was running for a United States Senate seat in Illinois against Stephen Douglas. The two men participated in a series of debates. In one of them Lincoln said of the decision: "I believe the decision was improperly made and I go for reversing it."[18] In the Court's opinion, Chief Justice Taney had alluded to the fact that if Congress wanted to overrule the decision, they had an avenue— amending the Constitution. Congress would later do just that.

For the moment, however, the Dred Scott decision was a judicial and historical disaster that would lead to civil war. As one historian wrote, "The rhetorical battle that followed the Dred Scott decision, as we know, later erupted into the gunfire and bloodshed of the Civil War."[19]

4

The Birth of the Fourteenth Amendment

Conflicts between pro and antislavery forces intensified after the *Dred Scott* decision. To make the situation worse, in 1859, abolitionist John Brown led a group of fifty men on an attack on a federal arsenal at Harpers Ferry, Virginia. Brown sought to capture enough ammunition and weapons to forcibly free the state's slaves. Although the government acted quickly to capture Brown and then hang him, many leaders in the South worried that abolitionist forces would stop at nothing to end slavery.[1] Brown's raid mobilized Northern antislavery sentiment. To many, Brown became a martyr for the crusade against slavery. Now the South feared that an abolitionist would be elected president with the wide support of the North and make a move to end slavery once and for all.

These fears seemed to become a reality when, in 1860, the Democratic party split in two. Stephen Douglas of Illinois received Northern support, while John C. Breckinridge won support from Southerners. The Republican party nominated Illinois lawyer Abraham Lincoln, who had already carved out a national reputation for himself in his 1858 battle against Douglas for a Senate seat.

John Brown led a group of fifty men on a raid of a federal arsenal at Harpers Ferry, Virginia.

War!

Thanks to the split in the Democratic party which divided votes between the two Democratic candidates, Lincoln was elected the first Republican president. As Lincoln prepared to enter the White House, the country was moving toward a profound crisis. Even before Lincoln took over, several Southern states began to secede from the Union and together they formed their own confederate government. South Carolina was the first to secede, followed by Mississippi, Florida, Alabama, Georgia, and Louisiana. By late 1861, there were a total of eleven Confederate States. Texas, Virginia, Arkansas, North Carolina, and Tennessee had joined the original six states.

As Abraham Lincoln was assuming the role of president,
several Southern states began to secede from the Union.

In April 1861, the nation plunged into a bloody Civil War after the confederates fired on Fort Sumter in Charleston, South Carolina. Before the war ended in May 1865, more than six hundred thousand would die.

Tragically, a few days after the South's surrender, on April 14, 1865, Confederate sympathizer John Wilkes Booth assassinated President Lincoln. Other leaders would have to take up the job of reuniting the nation and removing slavery from the South.

Rebuilding the Nation

When Congress convened on December 4, 1865, it faced a difficult task. The nation had just emerged from a bloody civil war and President Abraham Lincoln was dead. The new president, Southerner Andrew Johnson, opposed many of Congress's plans for the postwar nation.

The thirty-ninth Congress embarked on a plan to ensure that the nation would be restored without slavery. This period, from 1865 to 1877, is known as Reconstruction. During these years, as it worked to heal the wounds of the nation, the thirty-ninth Congress passed three amendments to the Constitution. Known as the Civil War amendments, they would result in what many people would call a second American revolution.

In December 1865, Congress met without representatives from the South. The Southern states were excluded because they had seceded from the Union and formed their own Confederacy. The vast majority of the members of Congress were Republicans from the Northern states. These men had to figure out how to readmit the Southern states to the Union.

The thirty-ninth Congress included several members who would be leaders in the passage of the Fourteenth Amendment. The framers of the

Fourteenth Amendment do not receive as much attention as the Founding Fathers who drafted the Constitution, but they too were strong leaders who performed well under dire circumstances.

One of those leaders was Thaddeus Stevens. Stevens, of Pennsylvania, was a successful lawyer and Congressman. He was born in Vermont with a twisted or "club" foot. This disability set him apart from his peers until he entered school. His handicap led Stevens to identify with those who were unfortunate and downtrodden.[2] He was a leading lawyer in the state of Pennsylvania. He won nine of the first ten cases he argued before the Pennsylvania Supreme Court. In one of his early cases he successfully helped a Maryland slaveowner recover a slave who had fled to Pennsylvania. This 1821 case left a bitter taste in Stevens's mouth. Only two years later he publicly proclaimed his devotion to the abolitionist cause.[3] He would spend the rest of his life working to end slavery and help the former slaves. He was quoted as saying, "I wish I were the owner of every Southern slave, that I might cast off the shackles from their limbs, and witness the rapture which would excite them in the first dance of freedom."[4]

Stevens became the leader of the so-called Radical wing of the Republican party. Radical Republicans wanted political equality for African Americans and hoped to punish the South for leaving the Union and starting the Civil War. Many African Americans considered Stevens a hero, second only to Abraham Lincoln. He defended all kinds of people who suffered discrimination, including American Indians, Seventh-Day Adventists (a religious group), Mormons, Jews, Chinese, and, of course, African Americans.[5] During the Reconstruction period, Stevens was in his seventies.

Thaddeus Stevens, a congressman from Pennsylvania, became the leader of the Radical wing of the Republican party.

He made numerous speeches in favor of the Fourteenth Amendment. He has been referred to as the "Father of Reconstruction." An ardent abolitionist, Stevens disliked the South and its pro-slavery stance with a burning passion. Fittingly, at his death, by his own request, he was buried in an African-American cemetery.

John Bingham, an Ohio Congressman, drafted what became the first section of the amendment. For this reason, twentieth-century Supreme Court Justice Hugo Black referred to him as the "Madison of the first section of the Fourteenth Amendment."[6]

John Bingham grew up in Cadiz, Ohio, where he was exposed to anti-slavery and abolitionist ideas. He worked for a newspaper editor who was an avowed abolitionist. Bingham also attended Franklin College, which was led by Reverend John Walker, one of Ohio's leading abolitionists. During college, Bingham befriended one of his classmates, Titus Basfield, who was a former slave.[7]

As a member of the thirty-ninth Congress, Bingham introduced several resolutions that eventually formed section one of the Fourteenth Amendment. President Ulysses Grant later appointed Bingham as minister to Japan, a position he held for twelve years.

Charles Sumner, a senator from Massachusetts, also took an active role in the Reconstruction

Charles Sumner helped lead a campaign that overturned school segregation in Massachusetts.

amendments. A graduate of Harvard Law School, he had worked under United States Supreme Court Justice Joseph Story, who doubled as a law professor. He went on to practice law in his home state. In 1859, he represented an African-American man whose daughter was denied the right to attend an all-white public elementary school. Sumner argued the case before the Massachusetts Supreme Court. He told the judges: "I begin with the principle that according to the spirit of American institutions, and especially of the Constitution of Massachusetts, all men, without distinction of color or race, are equal before the law."[8]

Despite his eloquent argument, Sumner lost the case of *Roberts* v. *Boston*. He did not end his crusade against racism, however. He helped lead a campaign that overturned school segregation in Massachusetts. As a member of the Senate during Reconstruction, his work in the Roberts case convinced him of the need for a Fourteenth Amendment. He remained a strong advocate for equality for African Americans in the Thirty-ninth Congress.

The Agenda of the Thirty-ninth Congress and the State of African Americans in the South

Bingham, Stevens, Sumner, and the other members of the thirty-ninth Congress had the daunting task of restoring the Union and providing protection for the newly won civil rights of African Americans. To that end, from December 1865 until January 1866, more than seventy amendments were introduced in Congress.[9]

But the death of slavery did not automatically mean the birth of freedom.[10] Many Southern whites worked hard to keep African Americans in a state of subjugation, as close to slavery as possible by law. They were subjected to physical terror, poverty, and unemployment. Congress tried to pass laws that would place African Americans in an environment where they would have as much equality as possible in white America. First, Congress passed the Thirteenth Amendment, ratified in December 1865. It outlawed slavery throughout the country. The amendment directly overruled the Supreme Court's decision in Dred Scott, which had safeguarded the institution of slavery. However, the amendment did not clearly state that African Americans could become citizens and enjoy rights equal to those of white Americans.

Congress realized it needed to do more than eliminate slavery. It had to ensure that African Americans would become full citizens. In 1866, Congress passed, over President Andrew Johnson's veto, the Civil Rights Act of 1866. This law declared that all persons born in the United States were citizens. The law provided that African Americans would enjoy the "full and equal benefit of all laws and proceedings for the security of person or property, as is enjoyed by white citizens. . ."[11]

Unfortunately, many Southern states had passed a series of their own laws, called Black Codes, designed to keep African Americans in second-class position in society. These laws, similar to slave codes that had existed before the Civil War, prevented African Americans from voting, serving on juries, holding certain jobs, owning or carrying firearms, or meeting together after sunset.

Proposing a New Amendment

On December 5, Thaddeus Stevens introduced an amendment that would outlaw all forms of racial discrimination. It read: "All national and state laws shall be equally applicable to every citizen, and no discrimination shall be made on account of race and color."[12] This amendment would have opened all public facilities, including schools, to both African Americans and whites. Although they had generally opposed slavery, many in the North were not willing to go this far.[13]

On December 6, John Bingham introduced a resolution whose language would later appear in section one of the Fourteenth Amendment. Bingham's resolution provided that Congress would have the power "to pass all necessary and proper laws to secure to all persons in every State of the Union equal protection in their rights, life, liberty and property."[14]

Many radical members of the thirty-ninth Congress believed that something more was needed to protect African Americans from discrimination—something more permanent that would prevent a later Congress from repealing the 1866 civil rights law.[15]

The main difference between a regular law and a constitutional amendment is permanence. Congress can amend, or change, an existing law by passing a bill by a simple majority. Amending the Constitution requires far more effort. It requires passage by two-thirds of the members of Congress, and then three-fourths of the states in order to approve the amendment. The members of the thirty-ninth Congress believed that the provisions of the 1866 civil rights law needed to be stated in a constitutional amendment. This would help lead to the Fourteenth Amendment.

The Joint Committee

The opposition to African-American freedom from white southerners convinced many members of Congress that tough action was needed. Congress and President Johnson clashed over how best to readmit the Southern states into the Union. Johnson favored a course of action that was lenient to the Southern states. He planned to pardon (forgive) Southern Confederates and restore their property, except for slaves. Under Johnson's proposal, announced in May 1865, all a former Confederate had to do to receive a pardon was to take an oath of loyalty to the Constitution and pledge support to a policy of emancipation.[16] Many members of Congress, especially the Radical Reconstructionists, favored something tougher that would punish the South. On December 4, 1865, Chairperson Thaddeus Stevens introduced a "resolution of great importance to the legislative history of the Fourteenth Amendment."[17] Stevens's proposal called for the creation of a joint committee of fifteen members of Congress, nine from the House and six from the Senate. This committee would have the power to readmit the Southern states into the Union. The joint committee would study how to treat the seceded states and how to provide better protection for African Americans. The joint committee was approved on December 12 by a vote of 133 to 36. The vote was strictly along party lines, 133 Republicans and 36 Democrats. No members from the Confederate states would be readmitted to Congress until after the joint committee had finished its report.[18]

The joint committee was composed of twelve Republicans and three Democrats. One historian wrote of this committee: "No other committee of Congress ever wielded the power of the Joint Committee on Reconstruction or left so permanent an imprint on the country's history."[19] On January 20, the joint committee considered an amendment similar to Bingham's proposal. In February, Bingham introduced another amendment that was similar to what would become section one of the Fourteenth Amendment.

On February 28, Bingham passionately argued that the purpose of the amendment was "to arm the Congress of the United States . . . with the power to enforce the bill of rights as it stands in the Constitution today."[20] Bingham asked, "Is the bill of rights to stand in our Constitution hereafter, as in the past five years within eleven States, (the Confederate states), a mere dead letter?"[21]

The joint committee released its report in late April 1866. It contained the proposed amendment. The amendment was printed in leading newspapers around the country on April 29. Sections one, two, four, and five appeared almost exactly as what would later become the Fourteenth Amendment. The committee's proposed section three would have prohibited anyone who assisted the Confederates from voting for members of Congress until July 4, 1870. The final version prohibited such people from being elected to Congress.

The committee also proposed a bill regarding the restoration of the political rights of the eleven Confederate states. The bill proposed that after the proposed amendment had become part of the

Constitution and after "any State lately in insurrection shall have ratified the same" the states could be read-mitted.[22] This provision made ratification of the amendment a condition that had to be met before a Southern state could be readmitted to the Union and into Congress.

Congress began debating the proposed amendment in May. Thaddeus Stevens said the amendment cor-rected the "defect" in the Constitution and the Bill of Rights because it imposed limits upon the states. Other members of Congress were adamantly opposed to the amendment. Representative William Edward Finck, a conservative Democrat from Ohio said,

> Stripped of all disguises, this measure is a mere scheme to deny representation to eleven States; to prevent indefinitely a complete restoration of the Union and perpetuate the power of a sectional and dangerous party [the Republican party].[23]

Finck and some other congressmen were upset that twenty-five states could amend the Constitution when there were thirty-six states. However, several other members of Congress did speak in support of the amendment. Bingham gave a lengthy defense of the amendment. He said that "flagrant violations" of individual rights had occurred in the states. The amendment, he argued, was necessary to remedy the "many instances of State injustice and oppression."[24]

The last speaker in the House on May 10 was Thaddeus Stevens. He gave a stirring speech about the need for the Fourteenth Amendment. He made a specific reference to a tragedy in Memphis, Tennessee, in which local police had killed forty-six African Americans after a dispute with some African-American ex-soldiers. Stevens said, "Let not these friends of secession sing to me their siren call of peace and good will until they can stop my ears to the screams and groans of the dying victims in Memphis."[25] Stevens emphasized the need for imposing tough penalties on those who had actively supported the Confederacy. In a vote taken after the Stevens speech, the House representatives passed the amendment by a vote of 128 to 37.

Next, the amendment went to the Senate. On May 23, Senator Jacob Howard spoke in favor of it. He argued that section one of the amendment would apply the first eight amendments of the Bill of Rights to the states. (The Ninth and Tenth amendments dealt with the relationship between the state and federal governments.) Howard said, "The great object of the first section of this amendment is, therefore, to restrain the power of the States and compel them at all times to respect these great fundamental guarantees."[26]

Senator Daniel Clark of New Hampshire proposed a measure to amend section three. His suggestion would more closely resemble the wording of the final version of the Fourteenth Amendment than the House's original draft. On May 29, the Senate voted 43-0 to strike the House version of section three, which would have prevented any former Confederates from voting until 1870. Many senators feared the House version would have prevented ratification in the South.[27]

Ratification

President Andrew Johnson opposed the Fourteenth Amendment. He believed Congress and its joint committee had exceeded their power. On June 22, Johnson wrote Congress that the amendment had been forwarded to the state governors. He emphasized that even though he was sending the amendment to the states, he did not support it. One leading newspaper wrote that Johnson's message amounted to a declaration of war on the amendment.[28]

Despite his staunch opposition, on July 19, 1866, President Johnson's home state of Tennessee became one of the first to ratify the Fourteenth Amendment. Just five days later, on June 24, Tennessee was readmitted into the Union. Connecticut and New Hampshire followed suit and ratified the amendment in July. However, other states rejected the Fourteenth Amendment. By March 1867, twelve out of thirty-six states had rejected the amendment. Some legislators in both the North and South considered the amendment a dangerous intrusion into the authority of the states. A legislative committee in Texas argued that the Fourteenth Amendment in effect repealed the Tenth Amendment, the one that reserves all powers not expressly granted to the federal government to the state governments.

Partly in response to the Fourteenth Amendment, Congress passed the Reconstruction Act of 1867. This was actually a series of related measures. The Reconstruction acts imposed military rule over all of the former Confederate states except Tennessee, since it had already been readmitted to the Union. These states were divided into several military districts to be governed by Union generals. The law required the Confederate states to hold conventions and write new constitutions. The states had to allow African Americans the opportunity to vote on the new constitutions. The states also had to ratify the Fourteenth Amendment before being readmitted to the Union. As historian Peter Irons wrote, "This was, pure and simple, government by gunpoint."[29]

In June, 1868, Arkansas, Alabama, Florida, Georgia, Louisiana, North Carolina, and South

Although President Andrew Johnson opposed it, his home state of Tennessee became the first state to ratify the Fourteenth Amendment.

Carolina finally ratified the Fourteenth Amendment and were readmitted to the Union. On July 21, 1868, Secretary of State William Seward certified that the Fourteenth Amendment had been ratified by the required number of states. Mississippi, Virginia, and Texas eventually ratified the Fourteenth Amendment and were readmitted to the Union.

The First Test

Even though Congress is the branch of government that passes laws, the judicial branch interprets them. After the states ratified the Fourteenth Amendment in 1868, the United States Supreme Court had to interpret its application. Although the Fourteenth Amendment was passed to provide protection for African Americans, the first test of the amendment came from white butchers in Louisiana. Several companies challenged a state law that gave two slaughterhouses control of all local business (a monopoly) in the city of New Orleans. The law required all cattle dealers and butchers to conduct their business with the Crescent City Livestock Landing & Slaughterhouse Company. Challengers claimed that the state-granted monopoly deprived them of their constitutional rights under the Fourteenth Amendment. They also argued that the monopoly violated their "privileges and immunities" as citizens of the United States, denying them equal protection of the laws and due process.

The Court's Reading

In the slaughterhouse case, the Supreme Court rejected these arguments. It ruled 5-4 that the state-created monopoly did not violate the Fourteenth Amendment. The five-member majority interpreted the Fourteenth Amendment's "privileges and immunities" clause very narrowly to apply only to "fundamental" rights "which belong of right to the citizens of all free governments."[1] The majority focused on the first sentence of the Fourteenth Amendment which provides: "All persons born or naturalized in the United States . . . are citizens of the United States and of the State wherein they reside." The court interpreted this sentence to mean that there were two types of citizenship—state citizenship and federal or national citizenship. The court then read the second sentence which said that no state would infringe on the privileges and immunities of citizens of the United States. According to the court, this sentence only prohibited states from abridging rights that citizens held as national citizens. The court reasoned that pursing a certain occupation was a privilege or immunity of state, not national, citizenship. The only rights that were privileges or immunities of United States citizenship were the right of access to the country's seaports, the privilege of the writ of habeas corpus, the right to petition the government, and a few limited others.

In effect, the court ruled that the Fourteenth Amendment did not apply the protections of the Bill of Rights to the states. To do so, the majority argued, would make the Supreme Court "a perpetual censor upon all legislation of the States." The majority determined that interpreting the Fourteenth Amendment to provide protection against state governments would be "a departure from the structure and spirit of our institutions."[2]

The ruling conflicted with the views of several leading framers of the amendment. These men had meant the "privileges and immunities" clause to extend the protections of the Bill of Rights to the states.

Dissenting

Justice Stephen Field wrote a dissenting opinion. In it he said that the majority's reading of the Fourteenth Amendment made it a "vain and idle enactment, which accomplished nothing."[3]

Justice Frank Murphy also wrote a dissenting opinion. He explained, "By the Constitution, as it stood before the war, ample protection was given against oppression by the Union, but little was given against wrong and oppression by the States. That was intended to be supplied by this amendment."[4]

Reaction to the Decision

The *Slaughter-House Case* decision was very controversial. It served to go against the clear intentions of the framers of the Fourteenth Amendment. A leading member of Congress during the adoption of the Fourteenth Amendment, Senator Jacob Howard, said in May 1866, "The great object of the first section of this amendment is, therefore, to restrain the power of the States and compel them at all times to respect these great fundamental guarantees."[5]

Despite such statements, the Supreme Court had severely limited the scope of the privileges and immunities clause. Not until much later would the court find another avenue to apply the protections of the Bill of Rights to the states through the Fourteenth Amendment—the due process clause.

The Incorporation of the Bill of Rights

Some historians have argued that the Framers of the Fourteenth Amendment never anticipated the "constitutional potential" of the first section of their amendment.[1] The language of the due process and equal protections clauses would come to dominate American constitutional law in the twentieth century.

Because the Supreme Court had interpreted the "privileges and immunities" language very narrowly in the *Slaughter-House Case,* the question remained whether the Fourteenth Amendment extended the protections of the Constitution to cases involving the states. The legal question was whether the rights in the first eight amendments to the Constitution were "incorporated" into the due process clause of the Fourteenth Amendment.

In the 1897 case of *Chicago, B & Q. R. Co.* v. *City of Chicago,* the United States Supreme Court determined that the due process clause of the Fourteenth Amendment required a state government to compensate (pay) a railroad for taking part of its land for public use. "Due protection of the rights of property has been regarded as a vital principle of republican institutions," Justice John Marshall Harlan wrote for the majority.[2]

In its 1925 decision, *Gitlow* v. *New York,* the United States Supreme Court interpreted the term "liberty" in the due process clause to include the First Amendment guarantees of freedom of speech and freedom of press. The case involved a socialist (a person who advocates collective or governmental ownership and distribution of goods in society) named Benjamin Gitlow who was charged by New York State officials with violating a law that prohibited "advocacy of criminal anarchy." Gitlow had published writings called "The Left Wing Manifesto" and "The Revolutionary Age." In these, he encouraged the overthrow of capitalist governments.

Gitlow argued that his conviction violated his First Amendment rights. He said his writings concerned only abstract principles. The majority of the Supreme Court disagreed, and termed his writings "direct incitement."[3] The justices believed his writings could lead people to try to overthrow the government.

Even though the Court rejected Gitlow's defense, it laid down the general principle that the Fourteenth Amendment did extend the First Amendment freedoms of speech and press to the states. The Court wrote that it assumed that those freedoms "are among the fundamental personal rights and 'liberties' protected by the due process clause of the Fourteenth Amendment from impairment by the States."[4]

Powell *v.* Alabama

In the 1932 case *Powell* v. *Alabama,* the United States Supreme Court threw out the convictions of nine African-American youths known as the Scottsboro

Boys, who were accused of rape by two white women. The defendants were tried and convicted by an all-white jury only a week after they were indicted. They received no advice from an attorney. The jury sentenced the youths to death. The Sixth Amendment provided counsel to defendants in federal courts, but people charged in state courts did not have the same rights.

In its decision, the Court cited the 1897 railroad case and the 1925 *Gitlow* decision as evidence that certain fundamental rights in the Constitution were protected against state action by the due process clause of the Fourteenth Amendment. The Supreme Court determined that the right to an attorney in a state capital case was a "fundamental" right.

The Court extended this right to counsel in cases other than the death penalty in 1961. In *Gideon* v. *Wainwright,* the Court ruled that the state of Florida had violated the Fourteenth Amendment by failing to provide an attorney for a poor man charged with burglary. The Court quoted at length from the Powell case. Its decision stated that "any person charged with a crime, who is too poor to hire a lawyer, cannot be assured a fair trial unless counsel is provided for him."[5]

Total Incorporation Theory

Justice Hugo Black argued vigorously in several cases that the framers of the Fourteenth Amendment intended for the first section of the amendment to make the Bill of Rights apply to the states. Black believed that John Bingham, Thaddeus Stevens, and other members of the joint committee had wanted to overrule the decision in *Barron* v. *Baltimore.*[6]

A majority of the justices of the United States Supreme Court has never embraced Hugo Black's total incorporation theory. However, the Court over a period of years did begin to incorporate different provisions of the United States Constitution selectively into the Fourteenth Amendment.

In its 1937 decision *Palko* v. *Connecticut,* for example, the Court reasoned that the Fourteenth Amendment did not prevent the state of Connecticut from appealing a criminal case and retrying a criminal defendant. Frank Palko was convicted of second-degree murder. The state of Connecticut then petitioned to retry Palko because the trial judge had left out certain evidence that would have led to a conviction on first-degree murder rather than second-degree murder.

In the federal court system, the Fifth Amendment prohibited federal prosecutors from trying a person more than once for the same crime. However, the Bill of Rights only applied as limitations on the federal government. The Supreme Court rejected Palko's argument that he faced double jeopardy by being retried for the same crime. The court, in an opinion by Justice Benjamin Cardozo, said that some provisions in the first eight amendments of the Bill of Rights are so "implicit in the concept of ordered liberty" that they must apply to the states.[7] The prohibition against double jeopardy was not one of those rights. Cardozo wrote: "Does it violate those 'fundamental principles of liberty and justice which lie at the base of all our civil and political institutions?' The answer surely must be 'no'." The Court explained, "The state is not attempting to wear the accused out by a multitude of cases with accumulated trials. It asks no more than this, that the case against him shall go on until there shall be a trial free from the corrosion of substantial legal error."[8]

The Supreme Court overruled the *Palko* decision more than thirty years later. In the 1969 case of *Benton* v. *Maryland* the Court called the guarantee against double jeopardy "fundamental," tracing it back to ancient Greece and Rome.

Duncan v. Louisiana

In 1968, the United States Supreme Court ruled that the Fourteenth Amendment guaranteed a jury trial to an individual charged in state court of the crime of battery. Gary Duncan, a young African American, was charged and convicted of simple battery for allegedly slapping a white youth on the elbow.

Duncan asked for a jury trial, but the trial judge denied his request. Duncan was convicted and sentenced to sixty days in jail and a $150 fine. He appealed his conviction, arguing that state officials had violated his constitutional rights by denying him a jury trial. The state of Louisiana argued that the Constitution did not require the state to give any criminal defendant a jury trial in a state court. The state of Louisiana also argued that it did not violate Gary Duncan's constitutional rights because he was convicted of only a so-called "petty" crime and was sentenced to only sixty days in jail.

The Supreme Court disagreed with the state of Louisiana, determining that the "Fourteenth Amendment guarantees a jury trial in all criminal cases which—were they tried in a federal court—would come within the Sixth Amendment's guarantee."[9] The Court traced the right to a jury trial all the way back to the Magna Carta of 1215, a document signed by King John I of England. In it the king promised not to violate certain rights of noblemen.

In Duncan v. Louisiana, *the Court traced the right to a jury trial back to the Magna Carta of 1215, shown here.*

In the federal court system, a crime was considered "petty" if the defendant faced less than six months in jail. In the *Duncan* case, the Supreme Court refused to lay down a general definition as to what distinguishes a petty crime from a serious crime. However, the High Court noted that Duncan's crime could have earned him up to two years in prison. The Court concluded that this was a "serious crime and not a petty offense."[10]

In a separate opinion, Justice Hugo Black reiterated his earlier position that the Fourteenth Amendment extended all of the provisions of the Bill of Rights to the states. However, Black declared that "I am very happy to support this selective process through which our Court has . . . held most of the specific Bill of Rights' protections applicable to the States to the same extent they are applicable to the Federal Government."[11] Black was pleased to see the Court moving slowly in his direction.

The effect of decisions such as *Gitlow, Powell* and *Duncan* is that the vast majority of protections in the Bill of Rights were absorbed by the Fourteenth Amendment and made to apply to the states. Through the process of selective incorporation, people in the United States are now afforded nearly as many constitutional protections from state and local officials as they have against federal officials. The vehicle through which this process occurred is the Fourteenth Amendment.

Procedural Due Process

Justice Felix Frankfurter wrote in 1945 that "the history of freedom is, in no small measure, the history of procedure."[1] Procedural due process means that the government must act fairly and reasonably when it affects a person's interests in life, liberty, or property. For example, government officials must ensure that someone convicted of a crime receives a fair trial before a jury.

Many cases of procedural due process involve people who have been charged with a crime. Procedural due process is obviously vitally important in a criminal case because a person's liberty and even life is at stake.

The Supreme Court has determined that the procedures that law enforcement officials follow with regard to a suspect must ensure fairness. If the conduct of the police officers is not fair, a conviction can be overturned.

Fair Process in Criminal Cases

A classic example is the case of *Rochin* v. *California.* In 1952, three deputy sheriffs in Los Angeles County, California, learned that Antonio Richard Rochin might be selling drugs. The three law enforcement officials entered Rochin's home. They forced open Rochin's bedroom door on the second floor.

Rochin was inside sitting partly clothed on the side of the bed with his wife. The officers saw two capsules next to a nightstand. When they asked to whom the capsules belonged, Rochin swallowed them.

The deputies then forcibly removed Rochin from his home and took him to a local hospital. They ordered hospital workers to pump his stomach to remove the capsules. The stomach pumping caused Rochin to vomit up the two capsules. The capsules contained morphine, a drug that was illegal without a prescription. The police charged Rochin with possession of morphine. He was convicted and sentenced to sixty days in jail. During his trial, Rochin objected to the capsules being admitted into evidence because of the way police had forced their way into his home and had the capsules forcibly removed from his stomach.

The Supreme Court reversed the conviction, finding that the conduct of the police violated the due process clause. "This conduct . . . shocks the conscience," the Court wrote.

> Illegally breaking into the privacy of the petitioner, the struggle to open his mouth and remove what was there, the forcible extraction of his stomach's contents . . . this course of proceedings by agents of government to obtain evidence is bound to offend even hardened sensibilities.[2]

The Court noted that matters of criminal justice are generally left to the states. However, the Court stated that it had a responsibility to make sure that the conduct of the local and state police did not go against national rules of fundamental fairness.

✎ Faulty Confession

The Supreme Court has ruled that the methods by which police obtain a confession from a suspect must be fair. Otherwise the confession cannot be admitted into evidence for use in court. In *Haley* v. *State of Ohio,* police arrested a fifteen-year-old African-American youth, John Harvey Haley, and accused him of murder. The police alleged that Haley served as look-out for two other youths who robbed a grocery store and killed the owner. The police took Haley into custody. Five or six police officers questioned him for five straight hours. Haley claimed that the officers beat him. During the questioning, Haley was not advised of his right to an attorney. Nor was he allowed to make a phone call.

After several hours, the police showed Haley what they said were confessions from the two other suspects. Eventually, Haley signed a written confession. After his confession was signed, a lawyer hired by his mother was twice denied admission to the jail. Police did not allow his mother to visit him until five days after he made his "confession." It was used in court to obtain a first-degree murder conviction for Haley and a sentence of life in prison.

The United States Supreme Court narrowly reversed the conviction by a 5-4 vote. "We do not think the methods used in obtaining this confession can be squared with that due process of law which the Fourteenth Amendment requires," wrote Justice William Douglas.[3] The Court said the conduct of the police was "callous" and "darkly suspicious." Douglas concluded that the police conduct during its intense questioning of Haley made an "empty form the due process of law for which free men fought and died to obtain."[4]

✎ Procedural Due Process Rights of Juveniles

The United States Supreme Court decided another important procedural due process rights case involving a fifteen-year-old in Gila County, Arizona. Law enforcement officials arrested Gerald Gault for allegedly making a lewd telephone call to a woman in his neighborhood. Six months earlier, Gault had been in trouble for being with a youth who had stolen a lady's wallet.

Officers took Gault into custody on June 8, 1964, without leaving a note for his parents, who were both at work. A juvenile court judge held a hearing the very next day. No transcript was made of this hearing. At later court proceedings, the different parties disputed the testimony. Gault testified that he had dialed for the lewd phone call but then handed the phone over to his friend. A police officer later claimed that Gault admitted making lewd remarks.[5]

After the hearing Gault was kept in detention for a few days rather than being sent home to his parents. The judge eventually held another hearing on June 15. At this second hearing, probation officers filed a "referral report" about Gault but did not disclose the report to Gault's parents. The juvenile court judge declared Gault "delinquent" and ordered him sent to an "industrial school" until he turned twenty-one. The woman who had initially called the police about the lewd phone call was not present at the hearing. The judge relied solely on the testimony of the arresting police officer and the report by the probation officers.

Gault's parents argued that they were not given sufficient notice to prepare for the June 15 hearing. They said they did not have enough time to hire an attorney for their son to fight the criminal charges

IN THE

Supreme Court

OF THE

State of Arizona

IN the Matter of

PAUL L. GAULT and MARJORIE GAULT,
father and mother of GERALD FRANCIS
GAULT, a minor,

for a Writ of Habaes Corpus.

No. 8549

APPELLANTS' OPENING BRIEF

AMELIA D. LEWIS
Counsel, Northern Chapter,
Arizona Civil Liberties Union
Attorney for Appellants

Received two copies of the within brief this............day of
November, 1964.

----

for the Attorney General

Filed in the Supreme Court of Arizona this................day of
November, 1964.

Clerk

1

The Gault *case dealt with the due process rights of juveniles.*

against him. They filed a petition to contest the juvenile court's ruling. At that hearing, the juvenile court judge testified he committed Gerald as a "delinquent" because he fit the definition of a "delinquent child" which was one who was "habitually involved in immoral matters."[6]

Under the state's juvenile court system, a youth did not have a right to an attorney, the right to confront or cross-examine witnesses, the right not to testify against him or herself, the right to a transcript of the hearing, or the right to appeal.

In its 1967 decision, the Supreme Court ruled that juveniles were entitled to many of the same procedural due process rights of adults in regular criminal proceedings in state or federal courts. The Supreme Court wrote that "due process of law is the primary and indispensable foundation of individual freedom." The Court added, "The essential difference between Gerald's case and a normal criminal case is that safeguards available to adults were discarded in Gerald's case."[7]

The Court determined that the procedure by which Gerald Gault was branded a delinquent and sent to a juvenile detention center violated the basic standards of due process. Gault and his parents had been denied several rights: the right of adequate notice; the right to counsel; the right to be informed of the privilege against self-incrimination; and the right to cross-examine witnesses. As a result the Supreme Court reversed the Arizona court's delinquency finding, in part because Gault's "confession" was obtained by a police officer "without counsel and without advising him of his right to silence."[8]

The Court's decision gave juvenile defendants many of the due-process rights held by adult defendants. Without the Fourteenth Amendment, juveniles would not possess the right of due process, which the Court defined as the "primary and indispensable foundation of individual freedom."[9]

Due Process Rights for Students

Public school students also have due-process rights. In 1975, the United States Supreme Court ruled in *Goss* v. *Lopez* that the due-process clause of the Fourteenth Amendment requires school officials to give notice and a hearing to students facing suspension.

The case came about after nine students at several high schools and junior high schools in Columbus, Ohio, were suspended for ten days for disruptive conduct during February and March 1971. One of the students, Dwight Lopez, was suspended after a disturbance in the lunchroom that led to damage of school property. Lopez argued that he was not involved in the lunchroom incident. He said he was only an innocent bystander. However, he was not allowed to explain why he was in the lunchroom.

Under Ohio law, school officials were allowed to suspend students without first giving them a hearing to contest the charges. Under the law, school officials only had to notify the student's parents within twenty-four hours and state the reasons for the discipline. The student could appeal the decision to the board of education and speak at the next board meeting. The board could then decide whether to reinstate the suspended student.

Lopez and other students challenged the Ohio law in federal court. They argued that the failure to grant them a hearing either before or immediately after the suspension violated their rights to procedural due process. The students argued that they had a liberty interest in their reputations and a property interest in their right to a public education. They claimed that the suspensions severely damaged their reputation with fellow students and teachers and would affect their opportunities for higher education.

The school officials conceded that the due process clause protects students who suffer a "severe determent or a grievous loss," such as permanent expulsion.[10] The state argued, however, that a ten-day suspension is not a severe enough punishment to bring the due process clause into play. School officials also argued that the schools must have some way to impose discipline flexibly to ensure a safe learning environment.

The Supreme Court ruled in favor of the students. The court determined that a ten-day suspension "is a serious event" for the punished student. It concluded that "at the very minimum," students facing suspension "must be given some kind of notice and afforded some kind of hearing." The Court explained that this notice and hearing should generally occur before the student is removed from school.[11]

The court recognized that schools did, indeed, face a challenging task in imposing discipline. It also agreed that school officials must sometimes impose immediate punishment in order to effectively run the school. However, the Court said that fundamental fairness requires that a student receive notice and a hearing:

> The prospect of imposing elaborate hearing requirements in every suspension case is viewed with great concern, and many school authorities may well prefer the untrammeled power to act unilaterally, unhampered by rules about notice and hearing. But it would be strange disciplinary system in an educational institution if no communication was sought by the disciplinarian

with the student in an effort to inform him of his dereliction and to let him tell his side of the story in order to make sure that an injustice is not done.[12]

The Court noted that its decision dealt with suspensions for less than ten days. Longer suspensions or expulsions might force school officials to "require more formal procedures," such as giving the accused student a chance to have an attorney and a holding more elaborate hearing.[13]

These issues are vitally important to public school students today. In recent years, many public schools have adopted so-called "zero-tolerance" policies in an effort to combat juvenile violence and drug use. Under these policies, schools impose long-term suspensions and even expulsions for first-time student offenders. The prevalence of zero tolerance policies underlines the importance of providing students with notice and a hearing before harsh disciplinary action may be taken. Without these elements of fairness, injustice could be common.

8

Substantive Due Process

In addition to ensuring fair procedures, the due process clause of the Fourteenth Amendment also protects individual liberty against laws that are unreasonable or irrational. Due process means not only providing a proper procedure, but also making sure that the reason underlying any law is rational. In other words, the due process clause is called the "substantive" component. Its provision is known as substantive due process.

Substantive due process means that the government may not pass laws that have an unreasonable purpose. For example, the government would violate substantive due process if it tried to regulate certain aspects of citizens' private lives, such as the right to use birth control or the right to take a certain job.

Lochner v. New York

In the early twentieth century, the Supreme Court used a theory of substantive due process to strike down laws that regulated the economy. In the 1905 case *Lochner* v. *New York,* the Court ruled that a New York law limiting the number of hours a baker could work each week violated due process.

An 1897 New York law limited the number of hours a baker could work to sixty hours a week or ten hours a day. Union representatives had successfully petitioned the state legislature to pass the law to protect the health of workers who had often been required to work very long hours. Joseph Lochner, owner of Lochner's Home Bakery in Utica, New York, challenged the law after he was fined for forcing an employee to work more than sixty hours in a week.

After New York's highest state court upheld the employment law, Lochner appealed to the United States Supreme Court. His lawyers argued that the law violated due process because it arbitrarily interfered with the liberty to contract. That is, it prevented Lochner from making a private contract with his employees that could state how long they would work.

The Supreme Court agreed with Lochner's argument by a narrow 5-4 vote. The Court viewed the law as a labor law, rather than a true health measure meant to protect bakers from dangerous conditions. The majority said the state had unreasonably interfered with "the freedom of the master and employee to contract with each other in relation to their employment."[1]

The majority believed the Court had a duty to review and strike down laws that interfered with free enterprise. Four justices, including John Harlan and Oliver Wendell Holmes, dissented. Harlan argued that the court should engage in judicial restraint. It should step back and not strike down a law enacted as a health measure.

Holmes's dissent was more colorful. He argued that the Fourteenth Amendment did not allow the Court to use its own judgment as to what was the best economic policy. Instead of looking to the Constitution for the legality of a law, he wrote that the majority's opinion had "perverted" the meaning of the word "liberty" with its decision. According to Holmes, reasonable people consider this law a health measure.[2]

The Supreme Court gradually moved away from the reasoning of the Lochner Court. In later decisions, the Court deferred to the legislature's judgment about laws that regulated labor matters.

Fundamental Rights of Parents

During the early part of the Twentieth century, the Supreme Court stepped in and struck down several state laws that regulated the economic and social lives of Americans. The Court also examined legislation that affected the fundamental rights of parents to bring up their children. In its 1923 decision *Meyer* v. *Nebraska,* the Supreme Court struck down a Nebraska state law that prohibited the teaching of any foreign languages.[3] The Court determined that the law was arbitrary and unreasonable. The law provided that no teacher in any school, public or private, could teach any language other than English to a student until the student reached the ninth grade. The law imposed a small fine and a thirty-day jail sentence on those teachers caught teaching foreign languages to children who had not completed the eighth grade.

Robert Meyer was convicted of violating the law after he taught German to a ten-year-old boy at Zion Parochial School in Hamilton County, Nebraska. The Nebraska courts upheld Meyer's conviction. The Nebraska Supreme Court said it was harmful for Americans to allow "foreigners" to educate their children in their native languages.[4]

The United States Supreme Court unanimously reversed the Nebraska Supreme Court's decision. The Court determined that the law was arbitrary and unreasonable. It said that knowledge of the German language was not harmful and could, in fact, be "helpful and desirable." The Supreme Court wrote that "the individual has certain fundamental rights which must be respected." It acknowledged that the states want to instill civic virtue and pride in its citizens, and seemed to acknowledge that the "unfortunate experiences" of World War I in which the United States had fought Germany had led the states to pass such laws. However, the law did not just target the German language because it also forbade the teaching of French, Spanish, Italian, and other "alien speech."[5]

Two years later, in *Pierce* v. *Society of the Sisters of the Holy Names of Jesus and Mary,* the Supreme Court struck down an Oregon law that prohibited parents from sending their children to private schools. The law provided that all children between the ages of eight and sixteen who had not completed the eighth grade had to attend public school. If a parent did not send his or her child to public school, the parent would be charged with a misdemeanor for each day their child missed of public school.

Two schools, a Catholic school called Society of the Sisters of the Holy Names of Jesus and Mary and a military school called Hill Military Academy, challenged the constitutionality of the Oregon law. They argued that it infringed on parents' Fourteenth Amendment due process rights to rear their children. The Supreme Court unanimously agreed, citing the *Meyer* case. The Court concluded that the Oregon law interfered with the parents' liberty to control the upbringing of their children in matters of education. The Court wrote that "the fundamental theory of liberty . . . excludes any general power of the state to standardize its children by forcing them to accept instruction from public teachers only. The child is not the mere creature of the state."[6]

These cases represented the kind the Court would examine under the Fourteenth Amendment's due process clause. After 1937, the Supreme Court began to shift its focus "from property rights to human rights."[7] In its decisions, the Court indicated that laws affecting regular economic policy would be presumed constitutional as long as they were rational.[8]

The Supreme Court established its so-called rational basis test to examine laws that involved ordinary commercial transactions. The court more closely examined laws that affected fundamental rights—those included in the Bill of Rights. Over time the Court determined that the due process clause of the Fourteenth Amendment protects many individual rights, including the right to marry and the right to have an abortion in the early stages of pregnancy. Although these rights are not explicitly mentioned in the Constitution, the Court determined that they are included within the meaning of the word "liberty" in the due process clause.

Right to Marital Privacy

By law, the state of Connecticut imposed criminal penalties on people who used birth control. The state also punished those who counseled others about using birth control. The law said that any person who used or aided another in using "any drug, medicinal article or instrument for the purpose of preventing conception" could be fined and subject to a sixty-day jail term. The state argued that the law was necessary to prevent promiscuous sex and illicit affairs. The state's attorney argued that by reducing access to contraceptives the law would cut down on extramarital sex.

Estelle T. Griswold, the Executive Director of the Planned Parenthood League of Connecticut, and others who gave information to married couples on the use of contraceptives, were fined $100 under the law. Griswold and others claimed that the state law violated their constitutional rights.

The United States Supreme Court agreed. In its 1965 decision, *Griswold* v. *Connecticut,* the Court ruled that the laws invaded a fundamental right of privacy that could be found or implied in several provisions of the Bill of Rights. In his main opinion for the Court, Justice William Douglas ruled that although the right to privacy was not specifically mentioned in the Constitution, several provisions in the Bill of Rights contained "penumbras" or "zones of privacy."[9] For example, Douglas reasoned that the First Amendment does not specifically mention a right to freedom of association. However, Douglas pointed out that many times the Court had protected a person's right to associate with the people of his or her choice. Douglas wrote that several provisions in the Bill of Rights deal with a right to privacy, including the Fourth Amendment which shields citizens from unreasonable searches and seizures. "Would we allow the police to search the sacred precincts of marital bedrooms for telltale signs of the use of contraceptives?" Douglas asked. "The very idea is repulsive to the notions of privacy surrounding the marriage relationship."[10]

Right to an Abortion

In 1973, the United States Supreme Court decided one of its most controversial cases, *Roe* v. *Wade.* The case determined that women have a due-process right to have an abortion. The case began in March 1970, when a young woman filed a lawsuit under the pseudonym

argued that these buffer zones infringed on their First Amendment rights to engage in political speech. In its most recent opinion, the Court upheld a Colorado law requiring protesters to stay at least eight feet away from people who were entering and exiting abortion clinics.[14]

The Supreme Court has heard other abortion cases after Roe. In 1989, the Court upheld several provisions of a Missouri law that regulated abortions. One provision prevented public employees from performing abortions at public hospitals. Another provision prohibited public funding of abortion counseling. Another part of the law required physicians to perform medical tests before giving a woman an abortion to determine whether the fetus was "viable" or capable of living outside the mother's womb.

A divided Court upheld these provisions in *Webster* v. *Reproductive Health Services*. It determined that a state could prohibit abortions at public hospitals because the state could choose not to subsidize or fund abortions. The court reasoned that this did not violate a woman's right to privacy because she could obtain an abortion at a private clinic. The Court also upheld the other provisions. It determined that the requirement of certain medical tests was reasonable. The Court quoted Roe for the proposition that after a fetus is viable, a state "may, if it chooses, regulate, and even proscribe, (prevent) abortion except where it is necessary" to save the life of the mother.[15]

To the surprise and anger of some, the Court did not overrule *Roe*. However, Justice Blackmun said he viewed the *Webster* decision as harming the rights of women. He wrote in a stinging dissent: "I fear of the future. I fear for the liberty and equality of the millions of women who have lived and come of age sixteen years since Roe was decided."[16]

However, opponents of abortion believed the Court did not go far enough.

Right of Parents to Control Visitation

In 2000, the United States Supreme Court examined a Washington state law dealing with visitation rights in *Troxel* v. *Granville*. The law provided that "any person" could petition a court for visitation rights at any time. The law gave courts the power to grant visitation whenever the court determined such visitation would "serve the best interest of the child." The court could order visitation even if the child's parent objected.

Tommie Granville and Brad Troxel had a relationship that produced two children. After the unmarried couple separated, the children lived with their mother, Granville. Troxel and his parents regularly visited the children and the children regularly stayed at the Troxel grandparents' home. However, after Brad Troxel died, Granville informed the Troxel grandparents that she wished to limit their time with the children to one visit per month. The grandparents sued for greater visitation rights. A trial court judge ordered Granville to allow the grandparents more time with the children.

Granville argued that the Washington visitation law infringed on her fundamental right under the Fourteenth Amendment due process clause to make important decisions regarding her children. The case eventually reached the United States Supreme Court.

The Supreme Court sided with Granville, not the Troxel grandparents, in *Troxel* v. *Granville*. The Court acknowledged that third parties, such as grandparents, often play vital roles in the lives of children. However, the liberty interest of parents to control the care and custody of their children "is perhaps the oldest of the fundamental liberty interests recognized by this Court."[17] The Supreme Court reasoned that parents have the primary role in the rearing of children. The Court described the Washington visitation law as "breathtakingly broad" because it could allow a judge to "disregard" decisions by fit parents regarding visitation.[18] The Court concluded that the due process clause prevents a judge from infringing on the liberty interests of parents in regard to rearing their children "simply because a state judge believes a 'better' decision could be made."[19]

Limits on Due Process

The Supreme Court has placed limitations on the use of the due process clause to remedy wrongs. In 1989, the High Court found no due-process violation in *DeShaney* v. *Winnebago County Department of Social Services*—a case with profoundly disturbing facts. Joshua DeShaney, a young boy from Wisconsin, was severely beaten by his father Randy and suffered permanent brain damage. The Winnebago County Department of Social Services (DSS) learned from the police and neighbors that Joshua had been beaten in the past by his father.

In January 1983, Joshua was taken to a local hospital with multiple bruises. After a doctor suspected child abuse, he notified the DSS. The DSS placed Joshua in the temporary custody of the juvenile court. The DSS also convened a "Child Protection Team" consisting of a doctor, police detective, psychologist, lawyer, and several DSS caseworkers. The team concluded that there was insufficient evidence of child abuse and returned Joshua to his father.

Unfortunately, Joshua returned to the emergency room at least two more times with suspicious injuries. Emergency room personnel contacted DSS about these injuries too. However, DSS failed to provide protection for Joshua.

Next, a DSS caseworker went to the DeShaney home, but was told Joshua was too ill to see her. DSS took no action in response. Then, in March 1984, Randy DeShaney beat his son so badly that he suffered permanent brain damage. The father was subsequently tried and convicted of child abuse.[20] Joshua's mother, who was divorced from the father, sued the DSS for violating Joshua's due-process liberty interests. She also argued that the DSS had a special duty to protect Joshua, since he had been in the care of DSS earlier. The United States Supreme Court disagreed. It ruled that the due process clause does not require a state actor to "protect life, liberty and property of its citizens against invasion by private actors."[21] The Court concluded that the due process clause protected Joshua from injury by the state, but not by his own father: "a state's failure to protect an individual against private violence simply does not constitute a violation of the Due Process Clause."[22]

Three justices dissented—William Brennan, Thurgood Marshall, and Harry Blackmun. Brennan wrote that a state could violate a person's due-process rights not just by acting but by failing to act—"inaction can be every bit as abusive of power as action."[23] He reasoned that the state had violated its duty to protect children who were suspected to be child-abuse victims.

Blackmun was more passionate in his separate dissenting opinion. He exclaimed, "Poor Joshua!" and said that the majority's decision represented a "sad commentary upon American life."[24]

The due process clause provides American citizens with great protection from governmental infringements on their liberty. However, the case of Joshua DeShaney shows the limits of the Constitution. The Fourteenth Amendment cannot provide protection to someone injured by a private individual, except in rare, special circumstances.

Right to Die

One of the most controversial due process issues today is physician-assisted suicide. In 1997, the United States Supreme Court ruled in *Washington* v. *Glucksberg* that a Washington state law prohibiting the assisting of suicide was constitutional. Several doctors

In the case of Cruzan v. Missouri *concerning Nancy Cruzan, shown here, the Court ruled that a competent person could refuse life-saving hydration and nutrition.*

and a group called Compassion for Dying challenged the Washington law. They argued that people have a liberty interest in assisted suicide. The doctors based their argument on the Supreme Court's 1990 decision in *Cruzan* v. *Director, Missouri Dept. of Health.* In the Cruzan case, the Supreme Court had ruled that the Fourteenth Amendment due process clause granted "a competent person a constitutionally protected right to refuse lifesaving hydration and nutrition."[25] The doctors in the Glucksburg case argued that the Cruzan case supported their argument. However, the Supreme Court disagreed. It saw a difference between refusing medical care and committing suicide. The Court wrote, "The decision to commit suicide with the assistance of another may be just as personal and profound as the decision to refuse unwanted medical treatment, but it has never enjoyed similar legal protection."[26] The Supreme Court cited a long tradition of laws banning assisted suicide. Clearly, the due process clause provides a great deal of constitutional protection and individual freedom. However, it is not the only clause in the Fourteenth Amendment that does this. Just as significant is the Fourteenth Amendment's equal protection clause.

Equal Protection

The Fourteenth Amendment's equal protection clause demands that individuals be treated equally under the law. This clause has been used often by African Americans and other historically disadvantaged minority groups to combat discrimination.

Racial Discrimination and the Civil Rights Cases

Much equal protection case law came out of attempts by African Americans to enjoy the same benefits as white people. In 1875, Congress passed the Civil Rights Act of 1875. This law tried to provide African Americans equal access to public accommodations. It provided that all people were entitled to "equal enjoyment of the accommodations, advantages, facilities, and privileges of inns, public conveyances on land or water, theaters, and other places of public amusement."[1] Congress passed the act because states and individuals throughout the country frequently discriminated against African Americans, denying them admission to inns, theaters, railroads, and other public places. Many states passed a series of so called Jim Crow laws that made

Jim Crow laws throughout the South created separate facilities for African Americans.

African Americans second-class citizens. These laws created separate facilities for every conceivable service and activity from restrooms to telephone books.

The United States Supreme Court was somewhat measured in its support for the rights of African Americans. In 1880, in the case of *Strauder* v. *West Virginia,* the Supreme Court struck down a West Virginia law that prohibited African Americans from serving on juries. The Court declared that the equal protection clause of the Fourteenth Amendment was designed to "protect an emancipated race and to strike down all possible legal discriminations" against African Americans.[2]

A few years later, the Supreme Court decided *The Civil Rights Cases,* a series of cases from Kansas,

Missouri, California, New York, and Tennessee. They involved African Americans who were suing because they had been denied admission to inns, theaters, and public transportation. The cases gave the Supreme Court an opportunity to uphold Congress's goal to rid American society of discrimination. It also provided the Court with the chance to "either legitimize or condemn racism in the area of public accommodations."[3] The legal question was whether Congress had the authority, under the Thirteenth and Fourteenth amendments, to pass the 1875 Civil Rights Act outlawing racial discrimination in public accommodations.

The Supreme Court ruled that Congress did *not* have the authority under the amendments to pass the Civil Rights Act. The High Court noted that the Fourteenth Amendment protected citizens from actions by state officials, not private individuals or corporations.

The actions at issue in these cases were simply "private wrongs" according to the Court. "It would be running the slavery argument into the ground to make it apply to every act of discrimination," said the Court. At one point in its ruling, the Supreme Court wrote, an African American "ceases to be the special favorite of the laws."[4]

Justice John Harlan was the only dissenter. He wrote that "the substance and spirit of the recent amendments of the constitution have been sacrificed by a subtle and ingenious verbal criticism." Harlan warned that the effect of the Court's decision would be to "enter upon an era of constitutional law when the rights of freedom and American citizenship cannot receive from the nation" sufficient protection.[5]

The Court's decision crippled the movement for equal rights for African Americans. One scholar claimed that the decision "set back the civil rights aspirations of African Americans for more than a century."[6]

Fifteen years later, the Supreme Court would further sanction discrimination by upholding a legal doctrine known as "separate but equal."

Separate But Equal: Plessy v. Ferguson

During the years after the Civil War, many states, especially in the South, passed a series of laws, called Jim Crow laws, to ensure that African Americans and whites remained separate, or segregated. The name Jim Crow came from a character in a minstrel show (a comic variety show). Jim Crow laws kept African Americans and whites from interacting in almost all social situations . . . from using the same restrooms, to swimming pools, to dining facilities, to transportation, and even to playing games like checkers. Legislators justified the laws by relying on a legal doctrine known as "separate but equal." They reasoned that as long as facilities were equal, there was nothing wrong with the facilities being separate. This line of reasoning conveniently ignored the fact that the facilities reserved for African Americans were far inferior to that of whites. African-American schools, for example, received far less funding from the states compared to white schools. They were often found to use outdated textbooks "handed down" by white schools and were taught in inadequate buildings.

In 1896, the Supreme Court ruled that a Louisiana Jim Crow law was constitutional. In doing so, the court upheld the "separate but equal doctrine" in the infamous case *Plessy* v. *Ferguson*. In 1890, the Louisiana legislature passed a law saying that African Americans and whites must use separate coaches when traveling in railroad cars. The law required the railroads to establish "equal but separate" facilities for African Americans and whites. It also provided that if an individual tried to ride in a coach designated for another race, the individual would be subject to a twenty-five dollar fine and twenty days in jail. The penalty applied to any railway employee who allowed African-American and white customers to ride together.

In June 1892, Homer Plessy decided to test the law by deliberately taking a seat in the train cabin designated for white passengers. Plessy was known as an "octoroon" because he had seven white great-grandparents and only one African American great-grandparent.[7] Plessy claimed he had a right to sit in the white cabin. However, the railroad employees forcibly ejected Plessy from the cabin and had him arrested.

Plessy actually wanted to be arrested. He and others wanted his case to help them challenge the Louisiana law. Plessy was a friend of Rodolphe Desdunes, leader of New Orleans' American Citizens' Equal Rights Association.[8]

The case made it all the way to the Supreme Court, which ruled against Homer Plessy. The majority of the court ruled that the "separate but equal doctrine" was constitutional.

The Court noted that laws requiring separation of the races "do not necessarily imply the inferiority of either race to the other." It said that many states had established separate schools for African Americans and whites, and that the states had forbidden African Americans and whites to marry. The Court concluded, "If one race be inferior to the other socially, the constitution of the United States cannot put them upon the same plane."[9]

Once again, Justice John Harlan, a man who grew up as part of a slaveowning family in Kentucky, was the only dissenter in this historic case. Even Justice Harlan, whose views were quite progressive for his time, was paternalistic in his discussion of race relations. He wrote that the white race was the "dominant race in this country," and even said that "it will continue to be for all time, if it remains true to its great heritage and holds fast to the principles of constitutional liberty."[10] However, Harlan still recognized the basic inequality of the Louisiana law mandating separation of the races. He wrote, ". . . in view of the constitution, in the eye of the law, there is in this country no superior, dominant ruling class of citizens. There is no caste (a system of rigid social separation) here. Our constitution is color-blind and neither knows nor tolerates classes among citizens. In respect of civil rights, all citizens are equal before the law. The humblest is the peer of the most powerful.[11]

Harlan even predicted that, in the future, society would regard the majority's decision "as pernicious as the decision" in the Dred Scott case.[12] He was right.

Brown v. Board of Education

In the *Plessy* case, the Supreme Court had justified the Louisiana Jim Crow law by relying on the fact that segregation was common in education. Appropriately, segregation would be successfully attacked in an education case too. The 1954 *Brown* v. *Board of Education of Topeka, Kansas* case was a consolidation of five cases from the states of Kansas, South Carolina, Virginia, and Delaware, and the District of Columbia. Each of the cases involved African-American schoolchildren who were being denied admission to all-white schools. The lead petitioner was Oliver Brown, who sought to enroll his eight-year-old daughter Linda in a public school in Topeka, Kansas.

In Brown v. Board of Education, *the plaintiffs fought for integrated schools and classrooms.*

Brown and the other plaintiffs claimed that the forced segregation in schools violated their Fourteenth Amendment right to equal protection. They argued that separate schools were not equal and could not be made equal. The defense, on the other hand, contended that Linda Brown and the other children's rights were not violated because they had every opportunity to attend a separate and equal school for African Americans.

A leading lawyer for many of the plaintiffs was Thurgood Marshall, counsel for the NAACP Legal Defense Fund. Marshall would later become the first African American justice on the United States Supreme Court.

The Court unanimously ruled in favor of Oliver Brown and the other parents. It stated that segregation in education did indeed violate the equal protection clause of the Fourteenth Amendment. "We conclude that in the field of public education, the doctrine of 'separate but equal' has no place," the Court wrote. "Separate educational facilities are inherently unequal."[13]

In its decision, the Court cited several psychological studies that showed how segregated schools imposed a "badge of inferiority" on minority students. Among these studies, the Court cited a study by Kenneth B. Clark, a highly regarded African-American social scientist. Clark tested African-American children in Philadelphia, Boston, and other communities by showing them white and African-American dolls. Overwhelmingly the African-American children preferred the white dolls, showing signs of self-rejection. Clark said, "I don't think we had quite realized the extent of the cruelty of racism and how hard it hit."[14] The Court cited Clark's findings as evidence that separating African Americans from whites infused African Americans with a sense of inferiority.[15]

Chief Justice Earl Warren worked for several months to convince his fellow justices of the need for a unanimous ruling in *Brown*.[16] At the time the United States was in the midst of a Cold War with the Soviet Union. Its image was very important in a struggle that pitted two ideologies against each other. By showing the United States was making progress in race relations, Americans could achieve a better standing among the other nations of the world. The decision remains perhaps the shining moment in Supreme Court history, and a jumping-off point for the civil rights movement that would change the nation in the 1950s and 1960s.

Interracial Marriage

For many years, states had passed laws prohibiting marriage between persons of different races. By 1967, sixteen states still had laws on the books that banned interracial marriages. Virginia's law provided that if a white person married an African-American person, the white person would be guilty of a felony.

Mildred Jeter, an African-American woman, and Richard Loving, a white man, were married in the District of Columbia in 1958. Shortly after they married, they moved back to their home state of Virginia. Mr. Loving was arrested for violating the so-called anti-miscegenation law that prohibited interracial marriage. A trial judge sentenced Loving to one year in jail, but agreed to suspend the sentence if the Lovings

In 1958, Richard Loving was arrested in Virginia for breaking a law that prohibited interracial marriage.

left the state and did not return for twenty-five years. The judge stated,

> Almighty God created the races white, black, yellow, malay (people of Malaysian or Indonesian descent) and red, and he placed them on separate continents. And but for the interference with his arrangement there would be no cause for such marriages. The fact that he separated the races shows that he did not intend for the races to mix.[17]

The Lovings took their case to the United States Supreme Court. They argued that the interracial marriage ban violated their rights to equal protection and due process under the Fourteenth Amendment. The state of Virginia argued that its law did not violate the equal protection clause because the law treated both African Americans and whites equally. In other words, the state argued that because the law punished both races, neither race could be considered disadvantaged. Attorneys for the state of Virginia used statements by various Reconstruction era congressmen to try to show that the framers of the Fourteenth Amendment did not intend for the amendment to allow interracial marriages. The state also argued that the Supreme Court's 1883 decision in *Pace* v. *Alabama* supported its reasoning. In *Pace*, the High Court upheld an Alabama law that imposed greater penalties on those who committed adultery with a member of another race than with a member of their own race.[18]

The Supreme Court rejected all of the state's arguments. It ruled that the law had an "invidious" purpose—the advancement of white supremacy: "There can be no doubt that restricting the freedom to marry solely because of racial classifications violates the central meaning of the Equal Protection Clause."[19] The Supreme Court also determined that the Virginia law violated the due process clause. It reasoned that "the freedom to marry has long been recognized as one of the vital personal rights essential to the orderly pursuit of happiness by free men."[20] The freedom to marry was a fundamental liberty interest.

Discrimination in Jury Selection

In 1986, the United States Supreme Court ruled in *Batson* v. *Kentucky* that the equal protection clause requires that a prosecutor in a criminal case not exclude potential jurors based on race.[21] In court, a group of citizens are called into a courtroom to serve as potential jurors. The process of selecting jury members is known as voir dire. Each side in the case is allowed to challenge the potential jurors and stop certain people from serving as jury members. There are two types of challenges: "for cause" challenges— eliminating someone because they reflect a bias that would not allow them to judge the case fairly—and peremptory challenges that eliminate someone for no reason at all.

The Supreme Court placed limits on peremptory challenges in the *Batson* case. James Batson, an African American, was charged with burglary and receipt of stolen property. In the case, the prosecutor used his peremptory challenges to strike all African Americans from the jury panel. On appeal, Batson's lawyers argued that using peremptory challenges to strike people of a certain race violates the equal protection clause. The High Court agreed that Batson was denied equal protection of the law. The Court reasoned that jurors and litigants have a right to be free from stereotypes rooted in historical prejudices.

Affirmative Action

Perhaps the most controversial issue with respect to race in America is affirmative action. Affirmative action refers to programs that seek to promote diversity by increasing minority enrollment at educational institutions or in areas of employment.

Affirmative action often divides Americans along racial lines. Many believe affirmative action is needed to ensure that minorities do not face continuing discrimination. In a famous 1965 speech President Lyndon B. Johnson said, "You do not take a man who for years has been hobbled by chains, liberate him, bring him to the starting line of race, saying 'you are free to compete with all the others,' and still justly believe you have been completely fair."[22] Others believe that affirmative action amounts to reverse discrimination because it simply turns the discrimination around, against the majority.

The Supreme Court first waded into these troubled waters in its 1978 decision *Regents of the University of California* v. *Bakke*. Allan Bakke, a white male, sued after he was denied admission to the medical school at the University of California at Davis. Bakke claimed that the school violated his right to equal protection because it admitted several minority candidates whose qualifications were beneath his. The university had a special admissions policy. Sixteen of one hundred slots were reserved for minority applicants.

In its ruling, the Court emphasized that the equal protection clause of the Fourteenth Amendment protects all persons, regardless of race or sex. "The guarantee of equal protection cannot mean one thing when applied to one individual and something else when applied to a person of another color," the Court wrote. "If both are not accorded the same protection, then it is not equal." The High Court reasoned that any racial classification is "inherently suspect." The university argued that its special admissions program was necessary to benefit those who had suffered general "societal discrimination" and to create a diverse student body. The Supreme Court ordered the school to admit Allan Bakke. The Court ruled that the "fatal flaw" in the school's admission policy was "its disregard of individual rights."[23] The Court, however, did not say that the school could not consider race as a factor in its admissions policy. It ruled that under a more "flexible" policy, a university could use race as one of many factors in its admission decisions.[24]

Gender Discrimination

The United States has had a long history of discrimination against women. Women did not even receive the right to vote until the ratification of the Nineteenth Amendment in 1920. In the nineteenth and through much of the twentieth century, the United States Supreme Court did not offer much relief to women who were seeking justice and equal protection under the Fourteenth Amendment.

The Supreme Court's Early Paternalistic Views

In 1872, the Supreme Court ruled that a woman did not have a Fourteenth Amendment right to earn a living as a lawyer. Myra Bradwell, a resident of Chicago, had petitioned the state of Illinois for a license to practice law. After she was rejected because of her sex, she filed a lawsuit. She argued that the Fourteenth Amendment's "privileges and immunities" clause protected her basic liberty right to earn a living as a lawyer. The courts rejected her claim.[25]

In 1948, several women, including Valerie Goesaert and Margaret Goesaert, challenged a Michigan law that prohibited women from being employed as bartenders unless they were related to the male owner of the liquor establishment. The women argued that the law violated equal protection because it treated women differently, based on whether they were related to the bar owner.

The Supreme Court upheld the law. The court first noted that the state of Michigan could prohibit all women bartenders. However, the Court admitted, "Michigan cannot play favorites among women without rhyme or reason." It concluded that the law did have a rational reason for treating women relatives of bar owners differently from other women. The Court said the legislature could reasonably believe that allowing women who were not related to the owner to bartend could present moral and societal problems. Women whose male relatives owned the bar could be protected from the "hazards" of working at the bar.[26]

Modern Rulings

In the 1970s, the Supreme Court began to apply the equal protection clause more strongly to gender cases. In 1971, for the first time, the Court ruled in favor of a woman who alleged that her equal protection rights had been violated by a law that discriminated by gender. The High Court overturned an Idaho law that preferred males over females for handling estates.[27] In 1973, the Supreme Court ruled that female military personnel should be entitled to claim their male spouse as a dependent for increased medical benefits.[28]

Just as some of the Court's early equal protection race cases involved white rather than African-American plaintiffs, many of the Court's equal protection sex cases

Justice Sandra Day O'Connor was the first woman appointed to the Supreme Court.

actually involved men rather than women. In 1982, the Supreme Court ruled that the Mississippi University of Women violated the equal protection rights of Joe Hogan when it denied his application to nursing school. Justice Sandra Day O'Connor, the first woman appointed to the Court, wrote that a state must have an "exceedingly persuasive justification" for a policy that classifies people based on their gender.[29]

The Mississippi University for Women argued that its policy for a "females only" admissions policy was to compensate for past discrimination against women. They argued that its policy was a form of educational affirmative action. However, Justice O'Connor noted that women had not been traditionally excluded from the nursing profession. Rather, O'Connor reasoned that the school's females-only policy "tends to perpetuate the stereotyped view of nursing as an exclusively women's job," O'Connor wrote.[30]

Similarly, in 1994, the Supreme Court ruled that a prosecutor had violated the equal protection clause by striking male jurors in a paternity and child support case. An Alabama prosecutor had used nine of its ten peremptory challenges (the trial judge normally determines the number of peremptory challenges in a given case) to remove male jurors. The prosecution argued that male jurors would be more sympathetic to the male defendant in a paternity and child support case. However, the Court reasoned that this line of reasoning represented "the very stereotype the law condemns."[31]

The Court noted that race and sex discrimination in jury selection harms litigants, the community, and the individual jurors who were wrongfully excluded. It stated that being on a jury, like voting, is an important way for the average citizen to participate in the American democratic system. "When persons are excluded from participation in our democratic processes solely because of race or gender, this promise of equality dims, and the integrity of our judicial system is jeopardized," the Court wrote.[32]

✎ *Single Sex Military School:* U.S. v. Virginia

In 1996, the Supreme Court ruled that the Virginia Military Institute (VMI), a military college, must admit women. Justice Ruth Bader Ginsburg, the second woman justice on the United States Supreme Court, cited the long history of sex discrimination in the country in her majority opinion. Classifications based on sex, Ginsburg wrote, can no longer be used to "create or perpetuate the legal, social, and economic inferiority of women."[33] The state of Virginia argued that single-sex education offers legitimate educational

In 1996, the Supreme Court ruled that the Virginia Military Institute was required to admit women as students.

benefits to students. The state also argued that admitting women would negatively affect three important aspects of the VMI program: physical training, the absence of privacy, and the adversarial approach.

The state hired expert witnesses who testified that men tend to prefer a competitive, adversarial environment, while women tended to prefer a more cooperative environment.

Finally, the state argued that it would create another single-sex school just for women called the Virginia Women's Institute for Leadership (VWIL). The state described this proposal as a "parallel program" that would give women equal opportunities.[34] Justice Ginsburg dismissed the state's arguments. She noted that similar objections had been made when women began applying to law schools, medical schools, and the federal military institutes. She concluded that the state's reasons were based on improper sweeping stereotypes. With respect to the separate school for women, Ginsburg noted that the facilities were unequal. "VWIL's student body, faculty, course offerings and facilities hardly match VMI's," she wrote.[35] Ginsburg compared the state's offer to create a separate school for women to a situation in Texas more than fifty years ago when an African American applied to Texas Law School. Because the state did not want to admit African Americans to the main law school, the state set up a separate law program for African American students. In its 1950 decision, *Sweatt* v. *Painter*, the Supreme Court ruled that the state of Texas had failed to show that the schools would be substantially equal.[36]

Ginsburg concluded that the plan offered by the state of Virginia with respect to VMI was the same as that offered by the state of Texas with respect to Texas

Law School. The Court determined that the state must admit qualified women to VMI to fulfill its constitutional obligation of "genuinely equal protection."[37]

Over the years since the Fourteenth Amendment was created, the equal protection clause has been applied in many different circumstances. It serves to ensure that people are treated fairly and not subject to discrimination. Simply stated, "the equal protection guarantee has become the single most important concept in the Constitution for the protection of individual rights."[38]

10

The Legacy of the Fourteenth Amendment

The Fourteenth Amendment revolutionized American constitutional law. Before its adoption the Bill of Rights only protected citizens from invasions of individual liberty by the federal government. The Fourteenth Amendment changed all that by extending the protections of the Bill of Rights to state and local government officials.

When the Constitution was first drafted, African Americans were considered slaves while women were treated as second-class citizens. Over time the Fourteenth Amendment was used in many cases to extend the rights and privileges of full citizenship to these groups who were not fully protected before.

Although the United States still has problems with race and sex discrimination, the Fourteenth Amendment has provided the constitutional means to achieve a great deal of social progress. It contains arguably the two most important phrases in American constitutional law: due process and equal protection.

Historian Eric Foner has written that the broad language of the Fourteenth Amendment "opened the door for future Congresses and the federal courts to breathe meaning into the guarantee of legal equality, a process that has occupied the courts for much of the twentieth century."[1]

Take a look at today's newspaper headlines and the hot-button issues in our nation. Among them are racial profiling, abortion rights, the right to die, affirmative action, and grandparent visitation rights. Many of these issues have been argued in the courts with legal arguments that touch on the provisions of the Fourteenth Amendment. There are plenty of pressing constitutional issues that arise in public schools—school dress codes, school prayer, evolution versus creationism, locker searches, drug testing, sexual harassment, and zero tolerance policies. All of these, too, involve the Fourteenth Amendment.

Without the Fourteenth Amendment, public school students could not sue for violations of their freedoms found in the Bill of Rights. Americans may not always take time to appreciate the Fourteenth Amendment, but without it, individual freedom would be at risk.

THE CONSTITUTION OF THE UNITED STATES

The text of the Constitution is presented here. All words are given their modern spelling and capitalization. Brackets [ ] indicate parts that have been changed or set aside by amendments.

Preamble

We the People of the United States, in Order to form a more perfect Union, establish Justice, insure domestic Tranquillity, provide for the common defence, promote the general Welfare, and secure the Blessings of Liberty to ourselves and our Posterity, do ordain and establish this Constitution for the United States of America.

ARTICLE I

The Legislative Branch

Section 1. All legislative powers herein granted shall be vested in a Congress of the United States, which shall consist of a Senate and House of Representatives.

The House of Representatives

Section 2. (1) The House of Representatives shall be composed of members chosen every second year by the people of the several states, and the electors in each state shall have the qualifications requisite for electors of the most numerous branch of the state legislature.

(2) No person shall be a Representative who shall not have attained to the age of twenty five years, and been seven years a citizen of the United States, and who shall not, when elected, be an inhabitant of that state in which he shall be chosen.

(3) Representatives and direct taxes shall be apportioned among the several states which may be included within this union, according to their respective numbers, [which shall be determined by adding to the whole number of free persons, including those bound to service for a term of years, and excluding Indians not taxed, three fifths of all other persons]. The actual Enumeration shall be made within three years after the first meeting of the Congress of the United States, and within every subsequent term of ten years, in such manner as they shall by law direct. The number of Representatives shall not exceed one for every thirty thousand, but each state shall have at least one Representative; [and until such enumeration shall be made, the state of New Hampshire shall be entitled to chuse three, Massachusetts eight, Rhode Island and Providence Plantations one, Connecticut five, New York six, New Jersey four, Pennsylvania eight, Delaware one, Maryland six, Virginia ten, North Carolina five, South Carolina five, and Georgia three].

(4) When vacancies happen in the Representation from any state, the executive authority thereof shall issue writs of election to fill such vacancies.

(5) The House of Representatives shall choose their speaker and other officers; and shall have the sole power of impeachment.

The Senate

Section 3. (1) The Senate of the United States shall be composed of two Senators from each state, [chosen by the legislature thereof,] for six years; and each Senator shall have one vote.

(2) Immediately after they shall be assembled in consequence of the first election, they shall be divided as equally as may be into three classes. The seats of the Senators of the first class shall be vacated at the expiration of the second year, of the second class at the expiration of the fourth year, and the third class at the expiration of the sixth year, so that one third may be chosen every second year; [and if vacancies happen by resignation, or otherwise, during the recess of the legislature of any state, the executive thereof may make temporary appointments until the next meeting of the legislature, which shall then fill such vacancies].

(3) No person shall be a Senator who shall not have attained to the age of thirty years, and been nine years a citizen of the United States and who shall not, when elected, be an inhabitant of that state for which he shall be chosen.

(4) The Vice President of the United States shall be President of the Senate, but shall have no vote, unless they be equally divided.

(5) The Senate shall choose their other officers, and also a President *pro tempore*, in the absence of the Vice President, or when he shall exercise the office of President of the United States.

(6) The Senate shall have the sole power to try all impeachments. When sitting for that purpose, they shall be on oath or affirmation. When the President of the United States is tried, the Chief Justice shall preside: And no person shall be convicted without the concurrence of two thirds of the members present.

(7) Judgment in cases of impeachment shall not extend further than to removal from office, and disqualification to hold and enjoy any office of honor, trust or profit under the United States: but the party convicted shall nevertheless be liable and subject to indictment, trial, judgment and punishment, according to law.

Organization of Congress

Section 4. (1) The times, places and manner of holding elections for Senators and Representatives, shall be prescribed in each state by the legislature thereof; but the Congress may at any time by law make or alter such regulations, [except as to the places of choosing senators].

(2) The Congress shall assemble at least once in every year, [and such meeting shall be on the first Monday in December], unless they shall by law appoint a different day.

Section 5. (1) Each House shall be the judge of the elections, returns and qualifications of its own members, and a majority of each shall constitute a quorum to do business; but a smaller number may adjourn from day to day, and may be authorized to compel the attendance of absent members, in such manner, and under such penalties as each House may provide.

(2) Each House may determine the rules of its proceedings, punish its members for disorderly behavior, and, with the concurrence of two thirds, expel a member.

(3) Each House shall keep a journal of its proceedings, and from time to time publish the same, excepting such parts as may in their judgment require secrecy; and the yeas and nays of the members of either House on any question shall, at the desire of one fifth of those present, be entered on the journal.

(4) Neither House, during the session of Congress, shall, without the consent of the other, adjourn for more than three days, nor to any other place than that in which the two Houses shall be sitting.

Section 6. (1) The Senators and Representatives shall receive a compensation for their services, to be ascertained by law, and paid out of the treasury of the United States. They shall in all cases, except treason, felony and breach of the peace, be privileged from arrest during their attendance at the session of their respective Houses, and in going to and returning from the same; and for any speech or debate in either House, they shall not be questioned in any other place.

(2) No Senator or Representative shall, during the time for which he was elected, be appointed to any civil office under the authority of the United States, which shall have been created, or the emoluments whereof shall have been increased during such time: and no person holding any office under the United States, shall be a member of either House during his continuance in office.

Section 7. (1) All bills for raising revenue shall originate in the House of Representatives; but the Senate may propose or concur with amendments as on other Bills.

(2) Every bill which shall have passed the House of Representatives and the Senate, shall, before it become a law, be presented to the President of the United States; if he approve he shall sign it, but if not he shall return it, with his objections to that House in which it shall have originated, who shall enter the objections at large on their journal, and proceed to reconsider it. If after such reconsideration two thirds of that House shall agree to pass the bill, it shall be sent, together with the objections, to the other House, by which it shall likewise be reconsidered, and if approved by two thirds of that House, it shall become a law. But in all such cases the votes of both Houses shall be determined by yeas and nays, and the names of the persons voting for and against the bill shall be entered on the journal of each House respectively. If any bill shall not be returned by the President within ten days (Sundays excepted) after it shall have been presented to him, the same shall be a law, in like manner as if he had signed it, unless the Congress by their

adjournment prevent its return, in which case it shall not be a law.

(3) Every order, resolution, or vote to which the concurrence of the Senate and House of Representatives may be necessary (except on a question of adjournment) shall be presented to the President of the United States; and before the same shall take effect, shall be approved by him, or being disapproved by him, shall be repassed by two thirds of the Senate and House of Representatives, according to the rules and limitations prescribed in the case of a bill.

Powers Granted to Congress

The Congress shall have the power:

Section 8. (1) To lay and collect taxes, duties, imposts and excises, to pay the debts and provide for the common defense and general welfare of the United States; but all duties, imposts and excises shall be uniform throughout the United States;

(2) To borrow money on the credit of the United States;

(3) To regulate commerce with foreign nations, and among the several states, and with the Indian tribes;

(4) To establish a uniform rule of naturalization, and uniform laws on the subject of bankruptcies throughout the United States;

(5) To coin money, regulate the value thereof, and of foreign coin, and fix the standard of weights and measures;

(6) To provide for the punishment of counterfeiting the securities and current coin of the United States;

(7) To establish post offices and post roads;

(8) To promote the progress of science and useful arts, by securing for limited times to authors and inventors the exclusive right to their respective writings and discoveries;

(9) To constitute tribunals inferior to the Supreme Court;

(10) To define and punish piracies and felonies committed on the high seas, and offenses against the law of nations;

(11) To declare war, grant letters of marque and reprisal, and make rules concerning captures on land and water;

(12) To raise and support armies, but no appropriation of money to that use shall be for a longer term than two years;

(13) To provide and maintain a navy;

(14) To make rules for the government and regulation of the land and naval forces;

(15) To provide for calling forth the militia to execute the laws of the union, suppress insurrections and repel invasions;

(16) To provide for organizing, arming, and disciplining, the militia, and for governing such part of them as may be employed in the service of the United States, reserving to the states respectively, the appointment of the officers, and the authority of training the militia according to the discipline prescribed by Congress;

(17) To exercise exclusive legislation in all cases whatsoever, over such District (not exceeding ten miles square) as may, by cession of particular states, and the acceptance of Congress, become the seat of the government of the United States, and to exercise like authority over all places purchased by the consent of the legislature of the state in which the same shall be, for the erection of forts, magazines, arsenals, dockyards, and other needful buildings;—And

(18) To make all laws which shall be necessary and proper for carrying into execution the foregoing powers, and all other powers vested by this Constitution in the government of the United States, or in any department or officer thereof.

Powers Forbidden to Congress

Section 9. (1) The migration or importation of such persons as any of the states now existing shall think proper to admit, shall not be prohibited by the Congress prior to the year one thousand eight hundred and eight, but a tax or duty may be imposed on such importation, not exceeding ten dollars for each person.

(2) The privilege of the writ of *habeas corpus* shall not be suspended, unless when in cases of rebellion or invasion the public safety may require it.

(3) No bill of attainder or *ex post facto* law shall be passed.

(4) No capitation, [or other direct,] tax shall be laid, unless in proportion to the census or enumeration herein before directed to be taken.

(5) No tax or duty shall be laid on articles exported from any state.

(6) No preference shall be given by any regulation of commerce or revenue to the ports of one state over those of another: nor shall vessels bound to, or from, one state, be obliged to enter, clear or pay duties in another.

(7) No money shall be drawn from the treasury, but in consequence of appropriations made by law; and a regular statement and account of receipts and expenditures of all public money shall be published from time to time.

(8) No title of nobility shall be granted by the United States: and no person holding any office of profit or trust under them, shall, without the consent of the Congress, accept of any present, emolument, office, or title, of any kind whatever, from any king, prince, or foreign state.

Powers Forbidden to the States

Section 10. (1) No state shall enter into any treaty, alliance, or confederation; grant letters of marque and reprisal; coin money; emit bills of credit; make any thing but gold and silver coin a tender in payment of debts; pass any bill of attainder, *ex post facto* law, or law impairing the obligation of contracts, or grant any title of nobility.

(2) No state shall, without the consent of the Congress, lay any imposts or duties on imports or exports, except what may be absolutely necessary for executing its inspection laws: and the net produce of all duties and imposts, laid by any state on imports or exports, shall be for the use of the treasury of the United States; and all such laws shall be subject to the revision and control of the Congress.

(3) No state shall, without the consent of Congress, lay any duty of tonnage, keep troops, or ships of war in time of peace, enter into any agreement or compact with another state, or with a foreign power, or engage in war, unless actually invaded, or in such imminent danger as will not admit of delay.

ARTICLE II
The Executive Branch

Section 1. (1) The executive power shall be vested in a President of the United States of America. He shall hold his office during the term of four years, and, together with the Vice President, chosen for the same term, be elected, as follows:

(2) Each state shall appoint, in such manner as the legislature thereof may direct, a number of electors, equal to the whole number of Senators and Representatives to which the State may be entitled in the Congress: but no Senator or Representative, or person holding an office of trust or profit under the United States, shall be appointed an elector.

(3) [The electors shall meet in their respective states, and vote by ballot for two persons, of whom one at least shall not be an inhabitant of the same state with themselves. And they shall make a list of all the persons voted for, and of the number of votes for each; which list they shall sign and certify, and transmit sealed to the seat of the government of the United States, directed to the President of the Senate. The President of the Senate shall, in the presence of the Senate and House of Representatives, open all the certificates, and the votes shall then be counted. The person having the greatest number of votes shall be the President, if such number be a majority of the whole number of electors appointed; and if there be more than one who have such majority, and have an equal number of votes, then the House of Representatives shall immediately choose by ballot one of them for President; and if no person have a majority, then from the five highest on the list the said House shall in like manner choose the President. But in choosing the President, the votes shall be taken by States, the representation from each state having one vote; A quorum for this purpose shall consist of a member or members from two thirds of the states, and a majority of all the states shall be necessary to a choice. In every case, after the choice of the President, the person having the greatest number of votes of the electors shall be the Vice President. But if there should remain two or more who have equal votes, the Senate shall choose from them by ballot the Vice President.]

(4) The Congress may determine the time of choosing the electors, and the day on which they shall give their

votes; which day shall be the same throughout the United States.

(5) No person except a natural born citizen, or a citizen of the United States, at the time of the adoption of this Constitution, shall be eligible to the office of President; neither shall any person be eligible to that office who shall not have attained to the age of thirty-five years, and been fourteen Years a resident within the United States.

(6) In case of the removal of the President from office, or of his death, resignation, or inability to discharge the powers and duties of the said office, the same shall devolve on the Vice President, and the Congress may by law provide for the case of removal, death, resignation or inability, both of the President and Vice President, declaring what officer shall then act as President, and such officer shall act accordingly, until the disability be removed, or a President shall be elected.

(7) The President shall, at stated times, receive for his services, a compensation, which shall neither be increased nor diminished during the period for which he shall have been elected, and he shall not receive within that period any other emolument from the United States, or any of them. "

(8) Before he enter on the execution of his office, he shall take the following oath or affirmation:—"I do solemnly swear (or affirm) that I will faithfully execute the office of President of the United States, and will to the best of my ability, preserve, protect and defend the Constitution of the United States."

Section 2. (1) The President shall be commander-in-chief of the Army and Navy of the United States, and of the militia of the several states, when called into the actual service of the United States; he may require the opinion, in writing, of the principal officer in each of the executive departments, upon any subject relating to the duties of their respective offices, and he shall have power to grant reprieves and pardons for offenses against the United States, except in cases of impeachment.

(2) He shall have power, by and with the advice and consent of the Senate, to make treaties, provided two-thirds of the Senators present concur; and he shall nominate, and by and with the advice and consent of the Senate, shall appoint ambassadors, other public ministers and consuls, judges of the Supreme Court, and all other officers of the United States, whose appointments are not herein otherwise provided for, and which shall be established by law: but the Congress may by law vest the appointment of such inferior officers, as they think proper, in the President alone, in the courts of law, or in the heads of departments.

(3) The President shall have power to fill up all vacancies that may happen during the recess of the Senate, by granting commissions which shall expire at the end of their next session.

Section 3. He shall from time to time give to the Congress information of the state of the union, and recommend to their consideration such measures as he shall judge necessary and expedient; he may, on extraordinary occasions, convene both Houses, or either of them, and in case of disagreement between them, with respect to the time of adjournment, he may adjourn them to such time as he shall think proper; he shall receive ambassadors and other public ministers; he shall take care that the laws be faithfully executed, and shall commission all the officers of the United States.

Section 4. The President, Vice President and all civil officers of the United States, shall be removed from office on impeachment for, and conviction of, treason, bribery, or other high crimes and misdemeanors.

ARTICLE III
The Judicial Branch

Section 1. The judicial power of the United States, shall be vested in one Supreme Court, and in such inferior courts as the Congress may from time to time ordain and establish. The judges, both of the supreme and inferior courts, shall hold their offices during good behaviour, and shall, at stated times, receive for their services, a compensation, which shall not be diminished during their continuance in office.

Section 2. (1) The judicial power shall extend to all cases, in law and equity, arising under this Constitution, the laws of the United States, and treaties made, or which shall be made, under their authority;—to all cases affecting ambassadors, other public ministers and consuls;—to all cases of admiralty and maritime jurisdiction, [—to controversies to which the United States shall be a party;—to controversies between two or more states, [between a state and citizens of another state;], between citizens of different states;—between citizens of the same state, claiming lands under grants of different states, and between a state, or the citizens thereof, and foreign states, [citizens or subjects].

(2) In all cases affecting ambassadors, other public ministers and consuls, and those in which a state shall be party, the Supreme Court shall have original jurisdiction. In all the other cases before mentioned, the Supreme Court shall have appellate jurisdiction, both as to law and fact, with such exceptions, and under such regulations as the Congress shall make.

(3) The trial of all crimes, except in cases of impeachment, shall be by jury; and such trial shall be held in the state where the said crimes shall have been committed; but when not committed within any state, the trial shall be at such place or places as the Congress may by law have directed.

Section 3. (1) Treason against the United States, shall consist only in levying war against them, or in adhering to their enemies, giving them aid and comfort. No person shall be convicted of treason unless on the testimony of two witnesses to the same overt act, or on confession in open court.

(2) The Congress shall have power to declare the punishment of treason, but no attainder of treason shall work corruption of blood, or forfeiture except during the life of the person attainted.

ARTICLE IV
Relation of the States to Each Other

Section 1. Full faith and credit shall be given in each state to the public acts, records, and judicial proceedings of every other state. And the Congress may by general laws prescribe the manner in which such acts, records, and proceedings shall be proved, and the effect thereof.

Section 2. (1) The citizens of each state shall be entitled to all privileges and immunities of citizens in the several states.

(2) A person charged in any state with treason, felony, or other crime, who shall flee from justice, and be found in another state, shall on demand of the executive authority of the state from which he fled, be delivered up, to be removed to the state having jurisdiction of the crime.

(3) [No person held to service or labor in one state, under the laws thereof, escaping into another, shall, in consequence of any law or regulation therein, be discharged from such service or labor, but shall be delivered up on claim of the party to whom such service or labor may be due.]

Federal-State Relations

Section 3. (1) New states may be admitted by the Congress into this Union; but no new states shall be formed or erected within the jurisdiction of any other state, nor any state be formed by the junction of two or more states, without the consent of the legislatures of the states concerned, as well as of the Congress.

(2) The Congress shall have power to dispose of and make all needful rules and regulations respecting the territory or other property belonging to the United States; and nothing in this Constitution shall be so construed as to prejudice any claims of the United States, or of any particular state.

Section 4. The United States shall guarantee to every state in this union a republican form of government, and shall protect each of them against invasion; and on application of the legislature, or of the executive (when the legislature cannot be convened) against domestic violence.

ARTICLE V
Amending the Constitution

The Congress, whenever two thirds of both houses shall deem it necessary, shall propose amendments to this Constitution, or, on the application of the legislatures of two thirds of the several states, shall call a convention for proposing amendments, which, in either case, shall be valid to all intents and purposes, as part of this Constitution, when ratified by the legislatures of three fourths of the several states, or by conventions in three fourths thereof, as the one or the other mode of ratification may be proposed by the Congress; provided [that no amendment which may be made prior to the year one thousand eight hundred and eight shall in any manner affect the first and fourth clauses in the ninth section of the first article; and] that no state, without its consent, shall be deprived of its equal suffrage in the Senate.

ARTICLE VI
National Debts

(1) All debts contracted and engagements entered into, before the adoption of this Constitution, shall be as

valid against the United States under this Constitution, as under the Confederation.

Supremacy of the National Government

(2) This Constitution, and the laws of the United States which shall be made in pursuance thereof; and all treaties made, or which shall be made, under the authority of the United States, shall be the supreme law of the land; and the judges in every state shall be bound thereby, anything in the constitution or laws of any State to the contrary notwithstanding.

(3) The senators and representatives before mentioned, and the members of the several state legislatures, and all executive and judicial officers, both of the United States and of the several states, shall be bound by oath or affirmation, to support this Constitution; but no religious test shall ever be required as a qualification to any office or public trust under the United States.

ARTICLE VII

Ratifying the Constitution

The ratification of the conventions of nine states, shall be sufficient for the establishment of this Constitution between the states so ratifying the same.

Done in convention by the unanimous consent of the states present the seventeenth day of September in the year of our Lord one thousand seven hundred and eighty seven and of the independence of the United States of America the twelfth. In witness whereof we have hereunto subscribed our Names.

Amendments to the Constitution

The first ten amendments, known as the Bill of Rights, were proposed on September 25, 1789. They were ratified, or accepted, on December 15, 1791. They were adopted because some states refused to approve the Constitution unless a Bill of Rights, protecting individuals from various unjust acts of government was added.

Amendment 1

Freedom of religion, speech, and the press; rights of assembly and petition

Amendment 2

Right to bear arms

Amendment 3

Housing of soldiers

Amendment 4

Search and arrest warrants

Amendment 5

Rights in criminal cases

Amendment 6

Right to a fair trial

Amendment 7

Rights in civil cases

Amendment 8

Bails, fines, and punishments

Amendment 9

Rights retained by the people

Amendment 10

Powers retained by the states and the people

Amendment 11

Lawsuits against states

Amendment 12

Election of the President and Vice President

Amendment 13

Abolition of slavery

Amendment 14

Civil rights

Amendment 15

African-American suffrage

Amendment 16

Income taxes

Amendment 17

Direct election of senators

Amendment 18

Prohibition of liquor

Amendment 19

Women's suffrage

Amendment 20

Terms of the President and Congress

Amendment 21

Repeal of prohibition

Amendment 22

Presidential term limits

Amendment 23

Suffrage in the District of Columbia

Amendment 24

Poll taxes

Amendment 25

Presidential disability and succesion

Amendment 26

Suffrage for eighteen-year-olds

Amendment 27

Congressional salaries

Chapter Notes

Chapter 1. The Second Bill of Rights

1. Eric Foner, *The Story of American Freedom* (New York: W. W. Norton & Company, 1998), p. xxi.

2. Howard Zinn, *A People's History of the United States: 1492-Present* (New York: HarperPerennial, 1995), p. 101.

3. John Paul Stevens, *Keynote Address: The Bill of Rights: A Century of Progress*, 59 U. Chi. L. Rev. 13, 22 (1992).

4. Fred W. Friendly and Martha J.H. Elliott, *The Constitution: That Delicate Balance* (New York: Random House, Inc., 1984), p. 25.

5. *Tinker* v. *Des Moines Independent Community School Dist.*, 393 U.S. 503, 506 (1969).

Chapter 2. The Five Sections of the Fourteenth Amendment

1. *Dred Scott* v. *Sandford*, 60 U.S. 393 (1857).

2. Howard Zinn, *A People's History of the United States: 1492–Present* (New York: HarperPerennial, 1995), p. 195.

3. John Hope Franklin and Alfred A. Moss, Jr., *From Slavery to Freedom: A History of African Americans* (New York: Alfred A. Knopf, 2000), p. 282.

Chapter 3. The Need for the Fourteenth Amendment

1. Leonard W. Levy, *Origins of the Bill of Rights* (New Haven: Yale University Press, 1999), p. 283.

2. Helen E. Veit, Kenneth R. Bowling, and Charlene Bangs Bickford, eds. *Creating the Bill of Rights: The Documentary Record from the First Federal Congress* (Baltimore: The John Hopkins University Press, 1991), p. 85.

3. *Barron* v. *City of Baltimore*, 32 U.S. 243 (1833).

4. Letter of Hezekiah Waters, April 2, 1817, in Fred W. Friendly and Martha J.H. Elliott, *The Constitution: That Delicate Balance* (New York: Random House, Inc., 1984), p. 3.

5. *Barron* v. *City of Baltimore*, 32 U.S. 247.

6. Ibid. 250.

7. Ibid. at 250–251.

8. Friendly, p. 15.

9. Howard N. Meyer, *The Amendment that Refused to Die: A History of the Fourteenth Amendment Revised* (Lanham, Md.: Madison Books, 2000), p. 35.

10. Peter Irons, *A People's History of the Supreme Court* (New York: Penguin Books, 1999), p. 157.

11. Ibid., p. 159.

12. Ibid., p. 160.

13. *Dred Scott* v. *Sandford*, 60 U.S. 393, 404 (1857).

14. Ibid., p. 537.

15. Ibid., p. 538.

16. Ibid.

17. Ibid., p. 564.

18. Meyer, p. 28.

19. Irons, p. 176.

Chapter 4. The Birth of the Fourteenth Amendment

1. Fred W. Friendly and Martha J.H. Elliott, *The Constitution: That Delicate Balance* (New York: Random House, Inc., 1984), pp. 216–217.

2. Fawn Brodie, *Thaddeus Stevens: Scourge of the South* (New York: W.W. Norton & Company, Inc., 1959), p. 26.

3. Ibid., p. 33.

4. Ibid., p. 63.

5. Ibid., p. 26.

6. Ibid., p. 371.

7. Richard Aynes, *The Anti-Slavery and Abolitionist Background of John A. Bingham*, 37 Cath. U.L. Rev. 881 (1988).

8. Ibid., pp. 14–15.

9. Joseph T. Sneed III, *Footprints on the Rocks of the Mountain: An Account of the Enactment of the Fourteenth Amendment* (San Francisco: TYSAM Press, 1997), p. 27.

10. Eric Foner, *The Story of American Freedom* (New York: W. W. Norton & Company, 1998), p. 104.

11. Howard Zinn, *A People's History of the United States: 1492–Present* (New York: HarperPerennial, 1995), p. 198.

12. Sneed, pp. 35–36.

13. Ibid., p. 36.

14. Ibid.

15. Howard N. Meyer, *The Amendment that Refused to Die: A History of the Fourteenth Amendment Revised* (Lanham, Md.: Madison Books, 2000), p. 56.

16. Sneed, p. 30.

17. Ibid., pp. 32–33.

18. Joseph B. James, *The Framing of the Fourteenth Amendment* (Urbana, Illinois: The University of Illinois Press, 1956), p. 39.

19. Brodie, p. 242.

20. Meyer, p. 86.

21. Sneed, p. 229.

22. Ibid., p. 323.

23. Ibid., p. 334.

24. Sneed, p. 363.

25. Brodie, p. 267.

26. Ibid.

27. Michael Kent Curtis, *No State Shall Abridge: The Fourteenth Amendment and the Bill of Rights* (Durham, N.C.: Duke University Press, 1986), p. 89.

28. Sneed, p. 383.

29. Joseph B. James, *The Ratification of the Fourteenth Amendment* (Macon, Ga.: Mercer University Press, 1984), p. 6.

30. Peter Irons, *A People's History of the Supreme Court* (New York: Penguin Books, 1999), p. 195.

Chapter 5. The First Test

1. *Slaughter-House Cases,* 83 U.S. 36, 77 (1873).

2. Ibid., at 78.

3. 83 U.S. at 96.

4. 83 U.S. at 129.

5. Joseph T. Sneed III, *Footprints on the Rocks of the Mountain: An Account of the Enactment of the Fourteenth Amendment* (San Francisco: TYSAM Press, 1997), p. 229.

Chapter 6. The Incorporation of the Bill of Rights

1. Joseph T. Sneed III, *Footprints on the Rocks of the Mountain: An Account of the Enactment of the Fourteenth Amendment* (San Francisco: TYSAM Press, 1997), p. 89.

2. 166 U.S. 226 (1897).

3. 268 U.S. 652 (1925).

4. Ibid. at 665.

5. *Gideon* v. *Wainwright,* 372 U.S. 335, 344 (1963).

6. *Adamson* v. *California,* 332 U.S. 46, 71–72 (J. Black dissenting).

7. *Palko* v. *Connecticut,* 302 U.S. 319 (1937).

8. Ibid., p. 328.

9. *Duncan* v. *Louisiana,* 391 U.S. 145 (1968).

10. Ibid. at 162.

11. Ibid. at 164 (J. Black, concurring).

Chapter 7. Procedural Due Process

1. *Malinski* v. *People of New York,* 324 U.S. 401, 414 (1945) (concurring opinion).

2. 342 U.S. 165 (1952).

3. Ibid., p. 598.

4. Ibid., p. 600.

5. *In re Gault,* 387 U.S. 1, 5-6 (1967).

6. Ibid., p. 8–9.

7. Ibid., p. 29.

8. Ibid., p. 55.

9. Ibid., p. 20.

10. *Goss* v. *Lopez,* 419 U.S. 565 (1975).

11. Ibid., p. 582.

12. Ibid., p. 581.

13. Ibid., p. 584.

Chapter 8. Substantive Due Process

1. *Lochner* v. *New York,* 198 U.S. 45 (1905).

2. Ibid., p. 76.

3. 262 U.S. 390 (1923).

4. Ibid., p. 397–398.

5. Ibid., p. 401.

6. *Gitlow* v. *New York,* 268 U.S. 510 (1925).

7. Ibid. at 535.

8. Peter Irons, *A People's History of the Supreme Court* (New York: Penguin Books, 1999), p. 333.

9. *Griswold* v. *Connecticut,* 381 U.S. 479, 484 (1965).

10. Ibid. at 485–486.

11. 160 *Roe* v. *Wade* 610 U.S. (1973).

12. Ibid., p. 163.

13. 410 *Roe* v. *Wade* 173 U.S. (1973).

14. *Hill* v. *Colorado,* 120 S.Ct. 2480 (2000).

15. *Webster* v. *Reproductive Health Services,* 492 U.S. 490 (1989).

16. Ibid. at 516

17. *Troxel* v. *Granville,* 530 U.S. 57, 65 (2000).

18. Ibid. at 67.

19. Ibid. at 73.

20. *DeShaney* v. *Winnebago County Dept. of Social Services,* 489 U.S. 189 (1989).

21. Ibid. at 195.

22. Ibid. at 197.

23. Ibid., p. 212.

24. Ibid. at 213.

25. Ibid., p. 279.

26. *Washington* v. *Glucksberg,* 521 U.S. at 725.

Chapter 9. Equal Protection

1. Eric Foner, *The Story of American Freedom* (New York: W. W. Norton & Company, 1998), p. 105.

2. *Strauder* v. *West Virginia,* 100 U.S. 303 (1880).

3. A. Leon Higginbotham, Jr., *Shades of Freedom: Racial Politics and Presumptions of the American Legal Process* (New York: Oxford University Press, 1996) p. 98.

4. 109 U.S. at 25.

5. 109 U.S. at 57.

6. Higginbotham, p. 106.

7. Peter Irons, *A People's History of the Supreme Court* (New York: Penguin Books, 1999), p. 222.

8. Ibid., p. 223.

9. 163 U.S. at 544, 552.

10. 163 U.S. at 559.

11. Ibid.

12. 163 U.S. at 559.

13. Ibid., p. 495.

14. Richard Kluger, *Simple Justice* (New York: Alfred Knopf, 1976) vol. 1 at p. 397–398.

15. *Brown,* 347 U.S. at 494–495.

16. Irons, p. 398.

17. *Loving* v. *Virginia,* 388 U.S. 1, 3 (1967).

18. *Pace* v. *Alabama,* 106 U.S. 583 (1883).

19. *Loving* v. *Virginia,* 388 U.S. at 12.

20. Ibid.

21. *Batson* v. *Kentucky,* 476 U.S. 79 (1986).

22. Howard Ball, *The Bakke Case: Education & Affirmative Action* (Lawrence, Kans.: University Press of Kansas, 2000), p. 12.

23. Ibid., pp. 289–290, 291, 306, 320.

24. Ibid. at 317–320.

25. *Bradford* v. *Illinois,* 83 U.S. 130 (1872).

26. *Goesaert* v. *Cleary,* 335 U.S. 464, 466 (1948).

27. *Reed* v. *Reed,* 404 U.S. 1 (1971).

28. *Frontiero* v. *Richardson,* 411 U.S. 677 (1973).

29. 458 U.S. 718 (1982).

30. Ibid. at 729.

31. *J.E.B.* v. *Alabama ex rel. T.B.*, 511 U.S. 127, 138 (1994).

32. Ibid. at 146.

33. 518 U.S. 515 (1996).

34. Ibid. at 534.

35. Ibid., p. 526.

36. Ibid. at 551.

37. 339 U.S. 629 (1950).

38. 518 U.S. at 557.

Chapter 10. The Legacy of the Fourteenth Amendment

1. Eric Foner, *The Story of American Freedom* (New York: W. W. Norton & Company, 1998), p. 105.

Further Reading and Internet Addresses

The Commission on the Bicentennial of the United States Constitution. *1791-1991: The Bill of Rights and Beyond.* Washington, D.C.: U.S. Congress, 1991.

Dudley, William, ed. *The Creation of the Constitution: Opposing Viewpoints.* San Diego, Calif.: Greenhaven Press, Inc., 1995.

Faber, Doris and Harold Faber. *We the People: The Story of the United States Constitution Since 1787.* New York: Charles Scribner's Sons, 1987.

Malone, Mary. *Andrew Johnson.* Berkeley Heights, N.J.: Enslow Publishers, Inc., 1999.

Weatherford, Carole Boston. *The African-American Struggle for Legal Equality in American History.* Berkeley Heights, N.J.: Enslow Publishers, Inc., 2000.

Internet Addresses

National Archives and Records Administration, *The Charters of Freedom,* "The Constitution: Amendments 11–27"
<http://www.archives.gov/exhibit_hall/charters_of_freedom/constitution/amendments_11–27.html>

National Archives and Records Administration, *The Charters of Freedom,* "The Constitution of the United States"
<http://www.archives.gov/exhibit_hall/charters_of_freedom/constitution/constitution.html>

National Constitution Center <http://www.constitution center.org/index.html>

Index